YORK FILM NOTES

Double Indemnity

Director
Billy Wilder

Note by Malcolm Kirtley

Longman

York Press

York Press
322 Old Brompton Road, London SW5 9JH

Pearson Education Limited
Edinburgh Gate, Harlow, Essex CM20 2JE, United Kingdom
Associated companies, branches and representatives throughout
the world

First published 2000

ISBN 0-582-43196-4

Designed by Vicki Pacey
Phototypeset by Gem Graphics, Trenance, Mawgan Porth, Cornwall
Colour reproduction and film output by Spectrum Colour
Printed in Malaysia, KVP

contents

acknowledgements Particular thanks to Mark Reid at the BFI for assistance with many aspects of the research.

—⫻—

author of this note Malcolm Kirtley has a long-held interest in film noir and the challenge the genre posed to established depictions of American society and individuals. He is Head of English at Wales High School in Rotherham and is General Editor of *English in Education*. He has previously edited *To the Lighthouse* in the Longman Literature Series.

background

trailer

Double Indemnity is sheer horror, so realistically conveyed by the characters of the story that it will put all those who see the picture on the Paramount Theatre screen under a nightmarish spell for days.

He [Billy Wilder] has taken the insidious development of a murder plan in the distorted brains of two people and and built it into the most terrifying study of crime and of the behaviour of criminals, that has ever reached the screen. He has done this with a tautness of direction that leaves the beholder breathless throughout exhibition of the film.

Kate Cameron, New York Daily News, 7 September, 1944

Billy Wilder has filmed the Cain story of the brassy couple who attempt a 'perfect crime' in order to collect some insurance, with a realism reminiscent of the bite of past French films. He has detailed the stalking of their victim with the frigid thoroughness of a coroner's report, and he has pictured their psychological crackdown as a sadist would pluck out a spider's legs. No objection to the temper of this picture; it is as hard and inflexible as steel.

Bosley Crowther, New York Times, 7 September, 1944

Double Indemnity tells a deliberate tale of murder with such eloquence, fluency and suspense that it is something more than a fascinating thriller. On more than one occasion it reaches the level of high tragedy.

Alfred Hitchcock has achieved the curious cinematic power which resides in *Double Indemnity* on several occasions. A foreign picture called 'M' had it. You will not find it often in Hollywood-made films.

Howard Barnes, New York Herald Tribune, 7 September, 1944

Double Indemnity is not a picture for Junior. And, just as definitely, the new arrival at the Paramount Theatre is about the most violent, startling and thoroughly absorbing melodrama seen hereabouts in a long time.

Enormously suspenseful, the picture holds its audience not so much by the story itself, but by the skilful manner in which it's spun out. And it's to director Billy Wilder and to scriptwriters Wilder and Raymond Chandler that credit goes for creating and sustaining a mood of mounting menace and impending doom.

Rose Pelswick, New York Journal, 7 September, 1944

Mr Wilder has made this a spine-chilling film, with incisive characterizations, occasional flashes of comedy, and always that brooding, terrifying atmosphere of murder.

Double Indemnity is not a picture to be easily forgotten. Its tale of murder, shocking and almost breathlessly exciting, has a curious fascination of its own.

Eileen Creelman, New York Sun, 7 September, 1944

Indemnity is rapidly moving and consistently well-developed. It is a story replete with suspense, for which credit must go in large measure to Billy Wilder's direction.

Variety Journal, 26 April, 1944

Taking a novel by James M. Cain – which must have owed a bit to the Ruth Snyder–Judd Gray murder case of some years back – Billy Wilder, director, and Joseph Sistrom, producer, have built up an unusual and powerful melodrama from as sordid a case of murder for insurance as has come to the screen. With the cast names of Fred MacMurray, Barbara Stanwyck and Edward G. Robinson for drawing power, and their uniformly excellent performances to

one of the greatest films of the film noir genre

sustain it, exhibitors may be assured they have a top attraction in the field of crime psychology.

E.A. Cunningham, Motion Picture Herald, 29 April, 1944

Double Indemnity excels as the perfect movie. For us movie enthusiasts, *Double Indemnity* is a landmark in the art of the cinema, in solid entertainment and everything else good that can be said of a motion picture.

Alton Cook, New York World Telegram, 6 September, 1944

reading double indemnity

The crisp direction, taut script, enigmatic lighting, brooding score and superb acting performances all combined to make *Double Indemnity* one of the greatest films of the film noir genre. Indeed, the seven Oscar nominations bestowed upon the film did much to elevate this previously perceived crude and morally ambiguous genre into the Hollywood mainstream. Subsequent years saw a burgeoning of the genre, linked to the commercial and critical success of Wilder's film.

Double Indemnity provides us with a central character and narrator who engrosses us in his sexual and financial seduction. Contemporary audiences would have been compelled to engage with Fred MacMurray, who plays Walter Neff, whose previous comic roles would have left them unprepared for the moral ambivalence of this film. We too are won over by his genial and affable persona and led into a moral complicity with a hero whose downfall achieves a pathos beyond melodrama. In Barbara Stanwyck, as Phyllis Dietrichson, we have a femme fatale perhaps unparalleled in the genre. Her seductive entrance and dominant sexuality create a unique frisson between herself and MacMurray which make his subsequent actions all the more plausible. In Edward G. Robinson as Barton Keyes, we have a doughty cynic whose caution and scepticism anchors the film in a tangible reality.

Wilder orchestrates a movie which never strikes a false note. Central to the film's success is the eloquent screenplay born from Wilder's fruitful, if painful, collaboration with Raymond Chandler. Together, they built upon the economies of Cain's prose with dialogue of such wit and panache that it manages to seamlessly bind the narrative whilst providing us with a series of memorable one-liners. Wilder's direction has a deceptive straightforwardness, as behind the apparent verity of his style lies a series of disturbing angles reminiscent of his background in German expressionism. The darkness which dominates the atmosphere in this sun-drenched city establishes a world of duplicity where actions occur in half-light and shadow. The editing reflects both the pace and the economy of the film, with even Neff's elaborate and expensively shot execution scene removed for the sake of narrative cohesion. Miklos Rozsa's score provides a brooding and dramatic accompaniment to the ongoing events.

Double Indemnity is memorable for taking the intrigue, duplicity and moral ambiguity of a popular tabloid genre, often serialised in pulp magazines, and creating a transformation of a popular but artistically complete motion picture. Many believed the film was unfilmable at a time when the Breen Office were particularly sensitive to any portrayals of moral ambivalence. The Second World War had helped to create the perception that moral certainties were more important than ever.

key players' biographies

BILLY WILDER (1906–)

Billy Wilder's work is a treasure trove of flesh and blood individuals, all wonderfully alive. In his canon of work are fall-down laughing comedies, stinging character studies, social satire, true suspense, aching romance ... the best in life, the sad and the giddy, the ironic and harrowing all have equal weight in his work.

Cameron Crowe, *Conversations with Wilder*, 1999, p. 11

Billy Wilder is one of the few remaining masters from the classic period of Hollywood film making. *Sunset Boulevard*, *The Lost Weekend*, *Some Like It Hot* and *The Apartment* are just some of his titles which have become key films in the Hollywood canon and which reflect the sheer diversity of his output.

His personal biography reveals a life expansive in its experience and which was touched by some of the key conflicts and movements of the twentieth century. He was born in Sucha, a town in Poland which was then part of Austria. His family moved to Vienna where he was educated, eventually becoming a successful journalist. Wilder was an independent spirit:

> I left my parents when I was 18 years old when I made the *Matura*, which is an exit exam, finishing high school. My father died in Berlin in 1928, and she was alone in Vienna.

Yet there was also personal tragedy:

> My mother died in the concentration camp, as did my stepfather, whom I never knew, as did my grandmother. They all died in Auschwitz, as I found out.
>
> *ibid., p. 121*

In 1926, Wilder moved to Berlin where he combined his journalistic work with screenwriting. In 1933, the Jewish Wilder fled Germany as Hitler came to power. He worked in Paris before moving to Los Angeles with a number of other émigré writers and directors. He was impressed by America and his first impressions remained with him:

> I first saw America from the Aquitania. We were delayed half a day, we were up in the harbor. It was a snowing winter night. I stayed with my brother in his little house in Long Island. In the morning when I got up, I looked out of the window. It was still snowing. And there was a big, black stretch Cadillac. Out comes a young boy with a stack of newspapers and he deposited one on the front doorstep. The weather was bad, and the newspaper boy's family was driving him in the big car. But to me, I thought, 'What kind of country is this?' Newspapers delivered by Cadillac! It was stunning! I liked it! I loved it!
>
> *ibid., p. 325*

biographies

The romanticism of this new country is there in his films, but so is a critical detachment which comes from his journalistic sensibilities. Indeed many regard his work as cynical, but the charge is difficult to sustain as ironic comedy imbues so many of his scripts.

Wilder began his Hollywood career as a scriptwriter and for several years experienced varying degrees of success on occasional collaborations. In 1938, he formed an unlikely pairing with Charles Bracket which lasted until 1950, by which time they had been responsible for some of the finest scripts of the late 1930s and 1940s. His desire for more creative autonomy and recognition of the importance of the director's role was apparent in 1942 when Wilder returned to directing in order to realise his scripts in a more controlled manner, with his collaborator Bracket as producer. Said Wilder:

> Bracket was a very loquacious man. He was kind of a member of the Alonquin Round Table. That was his milieu. He was a Republican, a rabid Republican. He was in the forefront of writers of the class of Hemingway, of Scott Fitzgerald – those were the people that he knew. And he learned very quickly ... because he wrote some stories for the Saturday Evening Post, and that's how he got into movies. And he was just kind of hanging around Paramount and did not know what the hell to do ... We had nothing in common except writing.
>
> *ibid., p. 40*

One of their biggest successes as writers was the script for Lubitsch's *Ninotchka*. The director was a mentor for Wilder whose work and approach was something he always admired: 'You know, if you could write Lubitsch touches, they would still exist, but he took that secret to his grave. It's like Chinese glass-blowing; no such thing exists anymore' (*Conversations with Wilder*, 1999, p. 357).

Wilder's success as a director was both critical and commercial. His films grossed over $100 million over his Hollywood career. He won Oscars as best director for both *The Lost Weekend* and *The Apartment*. He also won Oscars for the screenplays of *Sunset Boulevard* (1950), *The Apartment*

(1960) and *The Lost Weekend* (1945). Significantly, *The Lost Weekend* and *The Apartment* won Oscars as the best pictures of their respective years.

Wilder was one of Hollywood's most distinctive characters – 'a fast talking Middle European misanthrope with a riding crop' (Al Clark, *Raymond Chandler in Hollywood*, 1982) renowned for his splenetic manner. His writing collaboration with Chandler brought together two opposites who nevertheless produced a script on *Double Indemnity* of unparalleled vigour and economy. He was a pioneer in as much as he achieved success in a variety of genres and with *Double Indemnity* brought new quality to the hitherto underrated genre of film noir.

RAYMOND CHANDLER (1888–1959)

Raymond Chandler was fifty-five when he became involved in *Double Indemnity*. He was beginning to acquire a serious reputation as a novelist after a fertile four-year period in which four novels were published, beginning with *The Big Sleep* in 1939 and ending with *The Lady in the Lake* in 1943. His novels were separated from the pulp fiction of his contemporaries by their 'poetic toughness' and even Wilder, encouraged to read *The Big Sleep* by his producer, Joseph Sistrom, remarked 'anyone who can write like that is all right with me' (*Double Indemnity*, Richard Schickel, 1992, p. 32).

Chandler was not the streetwise cynic of his novels but a rather nervous academic. He had been educated at Dulwich College, an English public school, and served with the Canadian Armed Forces in the First World War. Between 1919 and 1932 he had a number of posts as a director of independent oil companies before losing his job in the depression. He never lost his affinity for England, where he felt writing, and screenwriting in particular, was more highly respected:

> I have just received a brochure about the Society of Authors, Playwrights and Composers in England and I am very interested to note that almost all the English screenwriters listed are either playwrights or novelists as well. Evidently, these people do not regard screenwriting as something only done by hacks or, when

'sex, debauchery, unpunished crime, sacrilege'

> done by writers of any reputation, done rather callously just for
> the money.
>
> *Letter to Joseph Sistrom, 16 December, 1947*

Chandler was clearly sceptical of the Hollywood style of collaborative
screenwriting and many of the resultant problems are documented later
(see Contexts: Production history). Al Clark's description of Wilder's first
meeting with Chandler anticipates many of the problems which would
stem from their divergent personalities:

> Wilder was astonished ... Expecting a tough, assured, witty
> wisecracker with the shoulders of a stevedore and a handshake
> like a pair of industrial pliers, he was instead confronted by this
> nervous, pallid academic, wearing a sports jacket with patches on
> the elbows and smoking a pipe.
>
> *Al Clark, Raymond Chandler in Hollywood, 1982*

As we will discover, Chandler was to claim that his involvement with Wilder
and the Hollywood system led to depression and alcoholism.

JAMES M. CAIN (1892–1977)

Cain was a former journalist who brought journalistic economies of style
to his writing. His bleak, almost existential world view made him one of
the key writers of the 'roman noir' movement (the French term for a type
of novel which deals with lowlife or sordid or corrupt subjects) and his
'hard-boiled' novels established a harsh realism. He started work as a
screenwriter in Los Angeles in 1931 and reflected his surroundings in three
novels, *The Postman Always Rings Twice*, *Double Indemnity* and *Mildred
Pierce*, which were regarded as 'the pictures they said could never be made'
because of their criminal, sexual and immoral content which went so
radically against the censorious power of the Breen Office and the
production code. Indeed, Edmund Wilson, who dubbed Cain 'a poet of the
tabloid murder', mourned his belief that the novels would never be brought
to the screen:

> All the things that have been excluded by the catholic censorship:
> sex, debauchery, unpunished crime, sacrilege against the church

- Mr Cain has let them loose in his stories with a gusto of pent-up ferocity that the reader cannot but share. What a pity that it is impossible for such a writer to create and produce his own picture!

Double Indemnity, 1992, pp. 19–20

A slight relaxation of the code eventually brought these 'unfilmable' novels to the screen and significantly it was Wilder and Chandler's deft adaptation of *Double Indemnity* which paved the way for the more notorious *The Postman Always Rings Twice.*

FRED MACMURRAY (1908–1991)

Fred MacMurray started his career as a band saxophonist and vocalist. He travelled with a variety of bands before a Broadway revue in 1930 and subsequently the musical *Roberta* led to his screen contract with Paramount. The affable MacMurray was largely identified with a series of light comic and romantic roles and as such his involvement in *Double Indemnity* was an inspired piece of casting. Wilder wanted 'a decent, bourgeois man' and the audience were predisposed towards empathising with his character, something essential to the moral ambiguity of the film. Kate Cameron wrote in the *New York Daily News*:

This is the first time MacMurray has had a chance to demonstrate his acting ability in a straight role and he upholds the judgment of director Wilder by turning in a top-notch performance of an average man who is led into committing a crime because of his crazy infatuation for a cold-blooded but insidiously sexy blonde.

Wilder recalls the casting of MacMurray in his recent interview with Cameron Crowe:

... there was an actor at Paramount, and he played comedies. Small dramatic parts, big parts in comedies. I let him read it and he said, 'I can't do that.' And I said, 'Why can't you?' He said, 'It requires acting!' I said, 'Look, you have now arrived in comedy, you're at a

Staid legitimacy versus
seductive duplicity

Wilder was extremely impressed by her acting ability

certain point where you either have to stop, or you have to jump over the river and start something new.' He said, 'Will you tell me when I'm no good?' And he was wonderful because it's odd casting.

Conversations with Wilder, 1999, p. 49

Surprisingly, MacMurray did not receive an Oscar nomination for what many regarded as his greatest performance.

BARBARA STANWYCK (1907–1990)

Barbara Stanwyck had a difficult upbringing. Orphaned at the age of four, she was brought up by her sister and family friends. She left school at thirteen and worked in a range of unskilled, low-paid jobs whilst training herself as a dancer. She began her career as a chorus girl at the age of fifteen and appeared with the 'Ziegfeld Follies' and other revues. Eventually in 1926, she got the lead in a straight play, *The Noose*, which had a nine-month run on Broadway.

Barbara Stanwyck's career reached a peak in the 1940s in films such as *The Lady Eve, Meet John Doe* and *Ball of Fire.* Indeed, in 1944 Ephraim Katz pointed out that the Internal Revenue Service announced she was the highest paid woman in America, slightly ahead of Bette Davis.

Stanwyck's earlier career as a chorus girl on Broadway and her portrayal of lower-class women had created associations with the less glamorous side of Hollywood – a past uniquely conducive here to her role as the archetypal femme fatale. She was respected as a committed performer. Wilder was extremely impressed by her acting ability and her professionalism:

She was just an extraordinary woman. She took the script, loved it, right from the word go, didn't have the agent come and say, 'Look, she's to play a murderess, she must get more money, because she's never going to work again.' With Stanwyck, I had absolutely no difficulties at all. And she knew the script, *everybody's* lines. You could wake her up in the middle of the night and she'd know the scene. Never a fault, never a mistake – just a wonderful brain she had.

Conversations with Wilder, 1999, p. 48

The great director Cecil B. De Mille was in agreement when he said, 'I have never worked with an actress who was more cooperative, less temperamental and a better workman.' Even the grudging New York critics had to acknowledge the quality of her work in *Double Indemnity*. Howard Barnes wrote in the *New York Herald Tribune*: 'Miss Stanwyck, who can often be a bit wooden, is vibrantly malignant and attractive as the homicidal wife' whilst Archer Winsten in the *New York Post* wrote with reluctant and rather tart praise: 'Stanwyck, long a person of no appeal and minimum acting talent to this reviewer, is beautifully equal to the demands of her role.' Whatever, her performance was enough to secure her an academy award nomination in a role still considered to be the archetypal femme fatale.

EDWARD G. ROBINSON (1893–1973)

Robinson was a marvellous character actor who came to fame for a series of roles in gangster movies during Warner's crime cycle of the 1930s. His first great success was as gangster boss Rico Bandello in *Little Caesar* (1931) and this led to his typecasting for several years in similar roles. In the 1940s, he began to expand his dramatic range and achieved success and acclaim in a variety of roles. After a series of roles as hard-boiled characters on the wrong side of the law, his role in *Double Indemnity* as the insurance investigator pursuing the truth provided a similar reversal of casting which again reflects the film's deliberate inversion of traditional moral codes and values.

Wilder described Robinson as 'a wonderful actor' and one who he rated as one of the screen greats along with Charles Laughton and James Cagney. He said that the great actors 'just do it' and he marvelled at the fact Robinson completed his memorable speech to Norton on the exhaustive possible methods of suicide in a single take.

Neff lights Keyes's cigar – a habitual gesture

The only genuine
relationship in the film?

director as auteur

The notion that the director is the auteur of a film provoked controversy in its assertion that the director was the organising source of meaning in a film when the process is a collaborative one, dependent upon the collective efforts of everyone involved, including actors, editors, producers and cinematographers. Most debate narrowed the primary creative forces of a film down to the director and the screenwriter. Some argued that without the script or scenario there was nothing, whilst others believed that the same script could be represented in radically different ways by different directors.

The debate was appropriate to Hollywood as the studio system with its influential producers was so dominant that the individual autonomy of directors could be questioned. Sarris saw the director as the primary exponent of cinematic art whose creative endeavours often rose above the profit-led studio bosses. However, in his definitive work on old Hollywood, Thomas Schatz argued that the entire Hollywood system was pivotal in the artistic and commercial success of that great period of movie making. The title of his book, *The Genius of the System*, comes from the cautionary words of French critic André Bazin to the early auteurists: 'The American cinema is a classical art so why not then admire in it what is most admirable – i.e. not only the talent of this or that filmmaker, but the genius of the system' (1998, p. 1).

It is interesting that Wilder found himself at Paramount which was regarded as a 'director's studio'. Although it had strong corporate managers, it did not have the archetypal executive producers, such as Louis B. Mayer at MGM or Darryl Zanuck at 20th Century Fox, both of whom had a major influence on film production. Thomas Schatz has shown how, 'Paramount's top talent enjoyed far more authority over the actual film-making process than their peers at the other major studios. Indeed, film-makers De Mille ... Ernst Lubitsch, Preston Sturges and Billy Wilder were the chief architects of Paramount's "house style".' (*The Cinema Book*, 1999, p. 13).

Wilder's desire for more creative autonomy and his recognition of the importance of the director's role led to his decision to direct his own

director as auteur

scripts. Whilst Wilder was relieved to achieve control as director, a man who had achieved so much through collaboration was unlikely to preciously perceive himself as an auteur. He was very matter of fact about his directorial skills and claimed he kept the process simple. Yet he did have discernible stylistic traits, as Richard Schickel eloquently observed in his study of *Double Indemnity*:

> he ... is powerfully drawn to night-for-day shooting; that is to say, rooms that are quite dimly lit even though we know the sun is shining outside. Chiaroscuro, shadow projections, shafts of bright light entering the frame at arresting angles – these are among Wilder's favourite devices.
>
> *1992, p. 10*

Schickel also points out how Wilder was direct in his style. He would not frame eccentrically or cut for faddish or shock effect. Yet he remains a key director and writer responsible for some of the most distinct but varied output in cinema history.

He was not a product of the system in as much as he had worked as a journalist and screenwriter in Berlin, before Hitler's rise to power in 1933 forced him to flee to Paris. His involvement with the creative freedom of the European film-maker clearly influenced his work with the major studios. With his co-writing credits and his imposing personality, Wilder was less susceptible to the dictates of the studios than many of his contemporaries. Indeed, Colin McArthur suggests that it was '"the sour and pessimistic sensibilities" of directors such as Lang Siodmak and Wilder "forged in the uncertainty of Weimar Germany and decaying Austria-Hungary" which provided the vital link between film noir and America in the 40s and 50s' (*The Cinema Book*, p. 186).

Wilder's autonomy and his contempt for some of the major bosses is captured in the following anecdote, based on an incident which took place after the first screening of Wilder's later film *Sunset Boulevard*, a biting satire on old Hollywood. Louis B. Mayer, head of MGM for twenty-seven years asserted: 'That Wilder! He bites the hand that feeds him!' to which Wilder replied, 'Mr Mayer, I'm Mr Wilder. Why don't you go and fuck yourself.'

Wilder reflected:

> He was astonished. He was standing with the great MGM bosses
> who were below him, there at the studio ... Mr Mannix and Joe
> Cohen. And that so astonished them that somebody had the guts
> to say, 'Why don't you go and fuck yourself' because I knew that I
> had a good picture there.
>
> *Conversations with Wilder, 1999, p. 255*

Such a splenetic retort to one of the most feared men in Hollywood
illustrates that Wilder was not suborned by the dictates of bosses. At the
same time, he was not a precocious individualist who dismissed all studio
requests. Indeed, he recently described himself as 'a company man' who
tried to protect the investment in a production, when reflecting on his
decision not to recast the lead actress in the film *Fedora* when the film was
not working.

narrative & form

defining film narrative

Narrative is a temporal sequence or as Christian Metz postulated: 'A doubly temporal sequence, one must hasten to specify: There is the time of the thing told and the time of the telling' (*Film Language, A Semiotics of the Cinema*, 1974, p. 18).

This basic but profound point about film narrative is perhaps the first thing we should recognise. Narrative is a system of temporal transformations which invents one time scheme in the sense of another. For example, as Metz pointed out, a summary montage sequence can capture three years of a hero's life in just a few seconds. Classical cinema attempts to make these temporal transformations as imperceptible as possible through techniques such as continuity editing which allows the focus to remain on character motivation and causal connections of cause and effect. Robert Stam, Robert Burgoyne and Sandy Flitterman-Lewis state:

> Classical cinema evokes the reconstruction of a fictional world characterised by internal coherence, plausible and linear causality, psychological realism, and the appearance of spatial and temporal continuity.
>
> *New Vocabularies in Film Semiotics, Structuralism, Post-Structuralism and Beyond,*
> *1992, p. 188*

They later go on to paraphrase David Bordwell, who has perhaps written more than any critic on aspects of classic Hollywood narrative:

> The classical Hollywood film, he argues, presents psychologically defined individuals as its principal causal agents, struggling to

'the causal logic of events unfolding in time'

> solve a clear cut problem or to attain specific goals ... the story ending either with a resolution of the problem or a clear achievement or non-achievement of the goals. Causality revolving around character provides the prime unifying principle.
>
> *ˈ1992, p. 189*

The anthropologist Levis-Strauss believed that plot was mere surface structure which concealed deeper logic and mythological meanings. However, theorists such as Prince and Propp believed that narrative was of far more structural importance in its ability to reveal the deeper meanings of a film or text:

> It does not simply mirror what happens; it explores and devises what can happen. It does not merely recount changes of state, it constitutes and determines them as signifying parts of signifying wholes ... Most crucially perhaps ... by discovering meaningful designs in temporal series ... narrative deciphers time ... and illuminates temporality and humans as temporal beings.
>
> *New Vocabularies in Film Semiotics, Structuralism, Post-Structuralism and Beyond, 1992, p. 70*

Thus narrative is not merely a passive reflection of story but the structural determiner of actions, events and relationships. Theories of narrative were often derived from the Russian formalist Propp who believed that 'the deep structure of narrative form consists precisely of the causal logic of events unfolding in time' (p. 80). His ideas were first applied to Russian wondertales where he discovered a universal system of organisation beneath all plot structure, which many film theorists subsequently applied to film narrative.

Propp discovered that the wondertales he analysed shared 'actions' or 'events' which could be represented in a table of thirty-one functions. The events always occurred in the same sequence, even though some could be left out of particular tales. He condensed the characters into seven archetypes who triggered particular roles in the plot. His seven tale roles were: the villain, the donor, the helper, the princess and her father, the dispatcher, the hero and the false hero. The functions and tale roles combined to create spheres of action. He separated tale roles from character, as characters could fulfil more than one tale role showing how the princess could also be the helper. He subdivided the overall structure into a set of moves, where several functions were linked together to represent a clear line of action and moves could follow consecutively or run parallel with one another.

Many critics have applied Propp's theory of narrative to film in an inventive and revealing manner. Others, such as Bordwell, are less enthusiastic, believing that Propp's model has been enforced in an inflexible and predetermined manner.

As we shall see in our analysis of the genre of film noir, there is evidence to show that a valid taxonomy of style and form can be built up around the body of films, and some of those features relate to narratology and character function. To what extent Propp's model can be applied to *Double Indemnity* is debatable. Wilder deliberately toys with our conception of tale role through casting and his particular style of 'telling'. Although Neff and Phyllis are the villains the audience are relieved along with the murderers when their faltering car finally starts and provides their getaway. Mr Dietrichson is a victim, yet a character so boorish and flawed that our sympathies are limited. Keyes is the hero in moral terms, but he is devoid of conventional romanticism and he is inherently suspicious of all human relationships. Even the dutiful daughter has an illicit relationship with the rebellious and hot-headed Zachetti. It is necessary to have a notion of existing roles to enable us to appreciate Wilder's deliberate deviance which foregrounds the ambivalent moral presentation. However, it is worth reminding ourselves of some of Culler's concerns on aspects of new criticism before particular theories are critically applied:

> ... a structuralism like Todorov's ... is accused of formalism: of neglecting the thematic content of a work in order to concentrate on its playful, parodic, or disruptive relation to literary forms, codes or conventions. On the other hand, critics who employ categories from psychoanalytical, Marxist, philosophical or anthropological theory are accused not of formalism but of pre-emptive or biased

> a normality which is disrupted by an event

> reading: of neglecting the distinctive themes of a work in order to find its manifestation of a structure or system prescribed by their system.
>
> *On Deconstruction, 1982, p. 20*

Such accusations can merely emanate from the conservative instincts of humanist critics but nevertheless the extent to which paradigmatic models are applied should always be considered carefully.

classic narrative structure

Noel Burch defined the codes which lay behind classic Hollywood Cinema of the 1930s and 1940s as the Institutional Mode of Representation (IMR). This consisted of 'techniques of mise-en-scène, framing and in particular editing, by means of which coherent narrative space and time are set up and fictional characters are individuated in ways which both engage, and are imperceptible to, the spectator' (*The Cinema Book*, 1999, p. 39).

It therefore seeks to disguise the cinematic structures and techniques through the illusion of naturalism. Editing was one of the principal means of achieving this.

The basic structure involves a normality which is disrupted by an event. That disruption has to be resolved before a new equilibrium can be returned to. The events which take place between disruption and final resolution constitute the narrative and they are ordered according to a logic of cause and effect. Events are driven forward by the motivations, actions and personalities of the central characters who are generally represented in a rounded manner. Classic narrative achieves a high degree of closure – there is a definite beginning, middle and end.

CLASSIC CODES OF NARRATIVE CINEMA

Annette Kuhn shows in her section on 'Classic Hollywood Narrative' in *The Cinema Book* how cinematic codes are formed from 'expressive resources' which can be used in various ways to drive narratives. The classic code shares the following features:

'Events proved you to be wrong'

1 Codes function to propel the narrative from the beginning to the resolution.

2 Causality is clear.

3 A credible fictional world must be created.

4 Credible characters with motivation and sustained human agency must inhabit that fictional world.

Kuhn shows how editing is vital in such cinema as events are ordered chronologically to set up causal links in time. Continuity editing creates 'invisible' links in the narrative so that temporal and spatial leaps can be accommodated by the viewer without disrupting their engagement with the narrative (see Style: Editing).

structure of double indemnity

Some interesting points on narrative structure in *Double Indemnity* can be found in Raymond Chandler's letter of December 1947 written to Joseph Sistrom, the Associate producer of *Double Indemnity* and Paramount's expert in contemporary fiction:

> ... Back in 1943 when we were writing *Double Indemnity* you told me that an effective motion picture could not be made of a detective or mystery story for the reason that the high point is the revelation of the murderer and that only happens in the last minute of the picture. Events proved you to be wrong, for almost immediately the mystery trend started, and there is no question but that *Double Indemnity* started it, although it was not exactly a mystery ... It is implicit in my theory of mystery story writing that the mystery and the solution are only what I call 'the olive in the martini', and the really good mystery is one you would read even if you knew somebody had torn out the last chapter.

We don't have to wait until the final scene to discover the identity of the murderer in *Double Indemnity* as Neff confesses within five minutes of his

exposition of motive, relationship and character

entry in the first scene. If this key element of surprise is removed from the mystery, then where does our engagement with the narrative reside? Clearly, it lies within the exposition of motive, relationship and character change and development, and it is this skilful manipulation of narrative which drives our interest and involvement.

Wilder has described the movements or spheres of actions in films as acts. For example number three of his top tips for writers is: 'If you have a problem with the third act, the real problem is in the first act' (*Conversations with Wilder*, 1999, p. 357). Even this wry statement shows the importance of a temporal order of cause and effect. The acts of *Double Indemnity* may crudely be divided in the following way, never forgetting that Neff's voice-over continually acts as a chronological interface:

Act I Normality disrupted by the meeting of Neff and Phyllis. Building to eventual sharing of joint motivation for murder.

Act II Planning and execution of murder.

Act III Aftermath and consequences of murder. Imminent threat of capture.

Act IV Increased discord between murderers as threat of discovery increases and final resolution.

Wilder's skilful use of some of the classic codes can be illustrated in the following sequence, stretching from the end of Neff's second visit to the Dietrichson household to his first meeting with Phyllis at his own apartment. Towards the end of Neff's second visit, he becomes aware of the true motives behind Phyllis's request to take out accident insurance on her husband in secret. His own 'little man' temporarily draws him out of his sexual infatuation with the realisation that he is 'not that crazy' to become embroiled in murder. Her coy fidgeting and evasive eye contact when making her request contrasts superbly with his unflinching gaze when he realises her motive.

His swift exit from the house instigates the first passing of time, marked by a dissolve from house to car. A further dissolve take us to the drive-in, where he attempts to calm down over a beer before another dissolve takes us to the bowling alley where he again tries vainly to take his mind off

highly skilful manipulations of narrative

Phyllis. A final dissolve, after Neff's car has disappeared into the car park below his apartment, takes us at dusk from the exterior window of Neff's apartment to his restless pacing inside.

All the time, this temporal and spatial summation has been complemented by Neff's voice-over, showing how incessant activity cannot provide the barrier to the inevitability of his fate. The passing of time has occurred in a credible manner, within the creation of a credible fictional world, and human agency and motivation has never strayed from the mind of the viewer.

Wilder takes us from summary or montage and back to scene once inside the apartment. The details of this scene will be analysed later, under mise-en-scène (see Style), but it is worth noting here some highly skilful manipulations of narrative. Phyllis has articulated her marital frustrations and murderous intent and Neff has attempted to show her the futility of her actions before finally, at the end of the first half of this scene, Neff tells Phyllis to 'stop thinking about it' in a rather unconvincing way.

The camera pans back before a dissolve takes us back to the present. The camera then pans in on Neff and his words, 'maybe she had stopped thinking about it, but I hadn't' revealing the flip side of his motivation for murder. From sexual obsession we are introduced to his economic and personal reasons for wanting to subvert the system which he currently serves. The camera emphasises his personal agenda by dramatically panning in and moving to close-up. The final and significant temporal and spatial shift occurs when the camera pans back from Neff and dissolves to Phyllis and Neff brooding on the sofa in his apartment. Fuelled by his additional motivation, Neff now asserts his aim.

Thus through the use of dissolve, summary and scene, Wilder has dramatically progressed the narrative and included a subtle but significant change of perspective. Contemplation and action have been enacted and the idea of human agency (against a backdrop of tragic inevitability) has been maintained. Phyllis's problem of the need for a helper (see Propp's ideas on pp. 22–3) has been resolved and complicated by Wilder through Neff's additional motivation, and this in turn prepares us for Act 2, the arrangements for the murder itself.

flashback & subjective narration

The single most important narrative device in the film is the sustained use of flashback which contextualises all events and imposes a unity of time, space and action. It fulfils a range of narrative functions, from ellipsis to summary to contextualising the very scenes themselves. On occasions, Neff's voice becomes the bridging music between one scene and another. The use of flashback involves depicting events in the present before retreating to the distant past and illustrating all that has occurred in-between before bringing the audience back to the present and some form of resolution. As such, it obeys a chronological order, albeit in reverse, and doesn't really involve more radical forms of non-linear expression. Narrative in *Double Indemnity* does not run off into parallel sub-plots since Neff remains our single point of view, even though on occasions we may question his reliability.

The use of flashback narration was an important generic feature of film noir (see Contexts: Generic classifications). Paul Schrader wrote it 'creates a mood of temps perdu: an irretrievable past, a predetermined fate, and an all-enveloping hopelessness'. The device is integral to the thematic coherence of *Double Indemnity* as Neff is indeed a figure without hope or a future whose fate is about to be pursued 'straight down the line'. As he sits rhythmically speaking into the dictaphone machine, struggling to light a cigarette, dry the sweat from his brow and stem the blood from his wound, we realise that escape is impossible.

opening credits

The opening credits are significant as they represent a pause in the narrative structure – that is they are outside of the time frame of the film but they none the less establish mood, expectation and a sense of foreboding. A male figure is seen walking haltingly on crutches towards the camera. His face is masked by his hat and an overcoat shrouds his body. Low-key lighting is used to create a silhouette and a shadow which grows to a monstrous size. Miklos Rozsa's music combines a slow march, which reflects the figure's ponderous movements, with a strident brass section, creating a sense of melodrama and portentous doom. Even at this stage the sense of duplicity and false identity is inferred as we wonder who the figure represents. Is it Dietrichson on his fateful journey to the car or Neff in imitation as he walks to the train carriage? Either way, this pause has successfully created a mood of fatalism.

opening

Before the subjective narration can begin, the film begins with an action sequence captured through an omniscient perspective and largely visual means. The film begins at night, or rather in the early hours of the morning. The camera fades into a downtown intersection. At the left and in the immediate foreground a traffic signal stands at go. A 1938 Dodge Coupe, a sporty if rather brash car, approaches in an erratic manner. When the signal changes to stop it makes no attempt to stop, causing a light newspaper truck to swerve and skid to avoid it. Already, the theme of lawlessness and ignoring conventional moral and authoritarian codes has been established. The car then careers down a small hill, and swerves to avoid the night workings of a team of workers for the Los Angeles railway, again a subtle allusion to Dietrichson's death on the rail tracks.

As the car pulls up outside the office building, the lights are turned off but for an instant nothing happens. A man eases himself out of the car and from his movements it is clear that something is wrong with him. He pulls the overcoat tight across his shoulders and walks towards the building. The title 'Pacific Building' sits above the plate glass doors and after knocking twice and thereby introducing a note of quiet desperation, the man is let in. There then follows a brief and vaguely comic turn of dialogue, with the comedy coming from the 'rheumatic' watchman. Neff, whom we later learn is quick-witted, is terse and monosyllabic here. As he leaves the elevator, the camera focuses on two glass doors containing the letters PACIFIC ALL-RISK INSURANCE CO. As Neff walks to his office, he is seen from the back and in shadow – again framing and lighting devices which are (or rather became – we must not forget the film's pioneering qualities) archetypal features of film noir. The camera follows his gaze down to the interminable rows of desks below where cleaners are tidying up after the working day. Even in this small shot and the wry smile that appears on Neff's face, we can trace the economic motives which lie behind his actions – his determination to rise above the mundanity of everyday working life by subverting the system which he serves. Neff is often viewed from the balcony, one step removed from the pen pushers below but still intrinsically part of their system and work ethic. It is not until he sits down and lights both his desk light and then a cigarette that we get a clear view of Neff – a withholding of identity which itself mirrors the duplicity involved in the murder itself.

The opening is an economic and highly effective piece of writing and directing, seamlessly moving us from the omniscient camera to the subjective voice of Neff as he picks up the dictaphone and begins the confession which both determines and punctuates the film.

close

The ending of *Double Indemnity* is significant as there were two main alternatives provided in the screenplay with Wilder eventually opting for the most economic of the two.

The first ending, adopted in the film, has Neff completing his final piece of subjective narration with a plaintive and regretful manner, trying in some way to compensate for the crimes he has committed:

```
It's almost four thirty now, Keyes. It's cold. I
wonder if she's still lying alone up there in that
house, or if they've found her by now. I wonder a
lot of things, but they don't matter anymore,
except I want to ask you to do a favour for me
Keyes. I want you to be the one to tell Lola, kind
of gently before it breaks wide open ... and I
want you to take care of her and that guy Zachetti
- so he doesn't get pushed around too much. Hello
Keyes ...
```

At this point the camera pulls back to the open door, returning us to a world of omniscient narration as the night watchman and the janitor peer curiously into the room over Keyes's shoulder. The badinage is exchanged but this time in a perfunctory, hollow manner. Neff's victory over Keyes's investigative skills is indeed an empty one and Keyes's admittance that 'you can't figure them all Walter' is delivered in an affecting manner. Neff expects the speech of condemnation but Keyes's reluctance to condemn his close friend is evident in his curt assertion that 'Walter, you're all washed up'. As Neff hopelessly begins his escape, he collapses by the glass doors before their final exchange:

Neff:

> You know why you couldn't figure this one,
> Keyes? I'll tell you. Because the guy you were
> looking for was too close, right across the
> desk from you.

Keyes:

> Closer than that Walter.

Neff:

> I love you too.

Neff's use of this phrase is delivered in an ironic, contrapuntal manner after Keyes had previously unburdened his frustrations over the incompetence of his colleagues. Here the words have a more poignant effect. Whether they suggest the homoerotic relationship perceived by some critics is debatable, but they do seem to hark back to some form of platonic ideal where male friendship and camaraderie could function without the taint of sexual attraction which has brought Walter down. Most significantly, as Walter fumbles to light his cigarette, Keyes takes the match, strikes it and lights it for him, a gesture which poignantly reciprocates Neff's earlier actions. The film ends with a visual symbol and motif, the final cigarette of the dying man in a moment of narrative unity.

Significantly, the scene concluded without Keyes lighting the cigarette and instead had Neff's word rhythmically trailing before the fade set in. In his

too bleak and unequivocal

preferred ending, Wilder allows an image and a gesture to represent character and theme more effectively than language.

SEQUENCE E

Sequence E was set in the witness room overlooking the death chamber in San Quentin jail. It was the most expensive scene in the film, rumoured to have cost $150,000 (although Wilder recently claimed it only cost $5,000) and yet it was removed from the final print. The three pages of script describing the scene are largely without dialogue and trace the process of the execution in minute detail:

```
E6 THE EXECUTIONER - MED SHOT - CAMERA SHOOTING DOWN
FROM HIGH ANGLE TOWARDS EXECUTIONER.

He pushes in metal lever. (This immerses the pellets
of cyanide in acid under the chair.)

INT. GAS CHAMBER - MED. SHOT

CAMERA IS SHOOTING ABOVE Neff's head (just out of
shot), towards spectators standing outside the gas
chamber, Keyes in the center. Gas floats up into
scene between CAMERA and spectators. Keyes unable to
watch, looks away.
```

Whether such a scene was included to placate the Breen Office by emphasising Walter's criminality is unclear, but it was certainly too bleak and unequivocal for a film imbued with ambiguity and ambivalence from the start. As shown earlier, the very casting of MacMurray as Neff was done to help us to identify and engage with his character, perhaps even to view him as Wilder preferred as 'a victim, not a murderer'.

Wilder's decision to remove this scene left him with a deft, succinct dénouement which enables Walter to reach his fatalistic conclusion, without losing the empathy from Keyes and the audience which is integral to the film's success.

Too bleak an ending for
a morally ambiguous film

character

NEFF

The significance of MacMurray's casting has already been alluded to and Wilder affirmed that 'he was wonderful because it's odd casting'. Neff's moral decline forms the basis for the narrative. Certainly his early exchanges would have conformed nicely to the audience's preconceptions. With both Phyllis and Keyes he is amusing and quick-witted, if a little corny and gauche. His early exchanges with Phyllis are rich with flirtatious double entendre, from the early 'I'd hate to think of your having a smashed fender or something while you're not fully covered' as she stands above, covered only by her towel, to the following famous exchange:

```
Neff:

     Wish you'd tell me what's engraved on that
     anklet.

Phyllis:

     Just my name.

Neff:

     As for instance?

Phyllis:

     Phyllis.

Neff:

     Phyllis. I think I like that.

Phyllis:

     But you're not sure?

Neff:

     I'd have to drive it around the block a couple
     of times.
```

His over-familiarity and flirtatiousness continues:

```
Phyllis:

     There's a speed limit in this state, Mr Neff.
     Forty-five miles an hour.
```

patterns which set the tone for their relationship

```
Neff:
     How fast was I going, officer?
Phyllis:
     I'd say around ninety.
Neff:
     Suppose you get down off your motorcycle and
     give me a ticket.
Phyllis:
     Suppose I let you off with a warning this
     time.
Neff:
     Suppose it doesn't take.
Phyllis:
     Suppose I have to whack you over the knuckles.
Neff:
     Suppose I burst out crying and put my head on
     your shoulder.
Phyllis:
     Suppose you try putting it on my husband's
     shoulder.
Neff:
     That tears it.
```

His speed of delivery is impressive, although significantly Phyllis finishes with the killer blow. Even in this short dialogue we see patterns which set the tone for their relationship.

Neff shows similar wit in his early exchange with Keyes, laughing at his affected grumpiness:

```
     You love it, only you worry about it too darn
     much, you and your little man. You're so darn
     conscientious you're driving yourself crazy.
     You wouldn't even say today is Tuesday unless
```

'forsaken the defence of ... hypocritical social order'

```
you looked at the calendar, and then you'd
check if it was this year's or last year's
calendar. And then you'd find out who printed
the calendar, and find out if their calendar
checked with the World Almanac's Calendar.
```

This wit changes radically at the end of the first act or sphere of action. Peter Evans detected an interesting link between Chandler's hero Phillip Marlowe and the character of Walter Neff in the film: 'Walter Neff represents the darker side of Phillip Marlowe. If Marlowe is a soiled Californian Galahad, tilting at the windmills of individual and corporate wickedness, Neff portrays the knight who has forsaken the defence of a dubious and hypocritical social order, deciding henceforth to strike out for himself' (*The Movie Book of Film Noir*, 1994, p. 167).

Neff's double motivation is apparent but his ultimate conformity and failure to unequivocally carry out the plan is evident from the start. After securing Mr Dietrichson's unknowing signature on the insurance certificate, he unwittingly ends up giving his daughter Lola a lift into town. His conformist values come through in his paternalistic approach to Lola and even Zachetti, and guilt is operating well before the act of murder takes place. He informs us: 'it gave me a nasty feeling to be thinking about them [Lola and Zachetti] at all, with that briefcase right behind my head that had her father's signature in it'. This neurotic guilt continues to manifest itself in his paranoid conversations with Phyllis in the supermarket. Here, the speed of delivery reflects nervous anxiety and not the quick wit of earlier conversations. He is brusque and awkward and his assertive commands are an attempt to disguise his growing unease and doubt which stand in sharp contrast to Phyllis's continued assurance:

```
Phyllis:
    Walter, I wanted ...
Neff:
    Not so loud.
Phyllis:
    I wanted to talk to you ever since yesterday.
```

nervousness and lack of conviction

Neff:

    Let me talk first. It's all set ...

Phyllis:

    But listen ... Walter

Neff:

    Open your bag quick.

After the act of murder, Phyllis's control ('No nerves. Not a tear. Not even a blink of the eyes ...') contrasts strongly with his guilt and anxiety. Yet he is elevated above the status of some naïve sap, seduced into murder through the machinations of a stronger woman, by the tragic role assigned to him:

    That was all there was to it. Nothing had
    slipped, nothing had been overlooked, there
    was nothing to give us away. And yet, Keyes,
    as I was walking down the street to the
    drugstore, suddenly it came over me that
    everything would go wrong. It sounds crazy,
    Keyes, but it's true so help me: I couldn't
    hear my own footsteps. It was the walk of a
    dead man.

In Act III (as Wilder labels events) Neff's nervousness and lack of conviction as the calculated murderer mounts. Keyes's investigative zeal makes him feel increasingly vulnerable and paranoid. His fear turns inward upon Phyllis and Neff's relationship and Phyllis's words at the end of this act have a portentous quality:

    Yes, I'm afraid. But not of Keyes. I'm afraid
    of us. We're not the same any more. We did it
    so we could be together, but instead of that
    it's pulling us apart, isn't it Walter?

Neff's friendship with Lola, which almost has conventional paternalistic qualities, once again reveals the essentially conformist soul which resides

Neff befriends Lola to keep her quiet

Lola's suspicions
lead Neff into
uncertainty and doubt

within him. Lola's assertion that Phyllis was responsible for her mother's death provides new dramatic tension creating further suspicion and mistrust between Neff and Phyllis. As Keyes later interviews Jackson in a brilliant moment of comedy which cuts against the prevailing mood of doom, Neff realises that their financial gain can no longer be pursued. His attempts to persuade her not to pursue her claim in court are rejected and Phyllis even retaliates with a threat reminding him of the pact they have entered into:

```
Phyllis:
     I only wanted him dead.
Neff:
     And I'm the one that fixed him so he was dead.
     Is that what you telling me?
```

Phyllis takes off her dark glasses for the first time and looks at him with cold, hard eyes.

```
Phyllis:
     And nobody's pulling out. We went into this
     together, and we're coming out at the end
     together. It's straight down the line for both
     of us. Remember?
```

Her resolve contrasts strongly with his anxiety. In the penultimate scene, her further machinations with Zachetti make Neff realise just how naïve he has been:

```
Phyllis:
     We're both rotten.
Neff:
     Only you're just a little more rotten ...
     Zachetti to take care of Lola, and maybe take
     care of me too ... That's the way you operate
     isn't it baby?
```

As these suspicions lead Phyllis to shoot Neff they hold one another in their symbolic deathly embrace. Whether the stony Phyllis softens in this final embrace is questionable. Certainly some critics see this as the only false moment in the film, as compared to Neff she has shown no delineation up to this point and her final speech appears to show uncharacteristic sentiment. Perhaps Wilder and Chandler once again wish to remove the audience from a fixed position as her words make Neff's actions all the more chilling:

Phyllis:

> No, I never loved you Walter. Not you or anybody else. I'm rotten to the heart.

Neff is no longer 'buying' her words, an interesting use of slang to capture the commodifying transformation of their relationship. Her agonised expression as she feels the gun at her side is one of the memorable moments in the film. Our sympathies may generally reside with the hapless, smarmy Neff but he nevertheless has killed two people in relatively cold blood. The first murder was committed out of our view as we focused on Phyllis's ecstatic, almost sexual response. Here, the deed is more evident and our sympathies are challenged. The classic pattern has been established where the assertive femme fatale has been punished for her attempts to challenge the patriarchy and here paid for it with her life. Yet Wilder complicates this as the 'victory' is clearly hollow as Neff will himself inevitably die and even Keyes we imagine will no longer get the same buzz out of his solution to this particular fraud.

PHYLLIS

The character of Phyllis Dietrichson is regarded as one of the archetypal femmes fatales. Her character role is to challenge the patriarchal status-quo but in her death we see a misogynist order reimpose itself (see Contexts: Generic classifications). It is interesting how Chandler and Wilder have elaborated the portrayal of Phyllis in the film. Cain's character of Phyllis Nirdlinger in the novel is one of unequivocal evil. From the moment Walter Huff enters her house we notice the ominous 'blood red Drapes', a symbol of her murderous intent manifested later in 'that red thing ... it's just one big square of silk that she wraps around her ... she looks what like came aboard the ship to shoot dice for the souls in the rime of the ancient mariner'. Cain's Phyllis has been responsible for the deaths of three children, in addition to the previous Mrs Nirdlinger and finally her own husband. She is a black widow and a macabre symbol of death in her final appearance before their joint deaths with her 'face chalk white, with black circles under her eyes and red on her lips and cheeks' (p. 114).

Such gothic intonations are never ascribed to Phyllis in the film. Her first appearance is one of sexual assertiveness and unconventionality as her appearance in her towel reveals her forwardness and disdain for propriety. Our focus on her partially clothed body is then replaced by the sight of her legs as she descends the stairway. The anklet, with its associations of prostitution, is a rather vulgar and obvious symbol of sexual licentiousness. The anklet becomes fetishised, her sexuality objectified. Yet her sexuality is never passive. She may be the subject of our voyeuristic gaze but like Manet's *Olympia*, she stares back. Phyllis is more than equal to Neff's banter and significantly gets the upper hand.

Her motives may be selfish and materialistic but like Neff she wishes to rise above the conformity of her life. Marriage is a trap which denies her autonomy and which imposes limits on her freedom:

> He's so mean to me. Every time I buy a dress or a pair of shoes he yells his head off. He never lets me go anywhere. He keeps me shut up. He's always been mean to me. Even his life insurance all goes to that daughter of his. That Lola.

Of course, we can't accept her words at face value as they may be subject to her scheming and manipulation. Dietrichson may be gruff and cantankerous but there is little evidence to support her accusations that he slaps her. Yet, the mise-en-scène of the family at the start of Act II deviates from Hollywood norms in its fragmentation and disharmony. Dietrichson lies exhausted, worn out by work and routine, whilst Lola seeks

'ice-cool, self-conscious and calculating evil'

escape from checkers with her detested stepmother which she asserts 'bores me stiff'. Phyllis clearly has reason to escape from this staid environment.

Peter Evans suggests that Phyllis's power goes beyond sexuality:

> ... in her metallic blondness, she is not the self-consciously sexual dark lady of her deadly sisters in the genre (Mary Astor, Jane Greer, Joan Bennet), but seems beyond sexuality, rather than of illicit passion. As the lighting, make-up, and costume combine to emphasise the negative ideological rhetoric of the femme fatale, Stanwyck's portrayal of ice-cool, self-conscious and calculating evil creates an image of such compelling egocentricity that it all but destroys the viewer's sympathy for Neff, Mr Dietrichson or any of the other men who may have been her victims.
>
> *1994, p. 169*

He later shows how she may 'perpetuate the myth of the female castrator' but she does challenge the status quo. Yet her ice-cool qualities are chilling. As the murder takes place, the camera stays in close-up on her unflinching gaze as she drives the car, and an expression of sexual fulfilment seems to come across her, reflecting some of the sadomasochistic elements which some critics have perceived in the film. After the murder her composure becomes one of the most significant character contrasts with Neff and dramatically it creates the tension and conflict that propels the narrative along. Neff comments: 'I was afraid that she would go to pieces a little, now that we had done it, but she was perfect. No nerves. Not a tear, not even a blink of the eyes.' This composure is most evident in the way she once again switches the power relations in her 'interrogation' by Norton where she once again leaves in control, having asserted control of the discourse:

```
Don't bother Mr Norton. When I came in here I
had no idea you owed me any money. You told me
you did. Then you told me you didn't. Now you
tell me you want to pay me a part of it,
whatever it is. You want to bargain with me,
```

an end which fulfils the demands of the code

> at a time like this. I don't like your
> insinuations about my husband, and I don't
> like your methods. In fact, I don't like you,
> Mr Norton. Goodbye, gentlemen.

Her impatience with Neff's indecision may lead to her further intrigue with Zachetti and her actions are clearly reprehensible, particularly the suggestion that she fuels the jealousy of Zachetti to the extent that he may in fact kill her. She does meet an end which fulfils the demands of the code and which imposes moral justice, but her interactions with less than noble men make her characterisation and her plot role more complex that it first appears.

BARTON KEYES

Edward G. Robinson provides one of the strongest performances in the film as Barton Keyes. His tale role as the doughty claims investigator would perhaps conventionally be carried out by a policeman. When Cain was researching his novel, he found that insurance claims investigators were often more tenacious than established police services as they had a vested financial interest in detecting any irregularities or fraudulent activity. His very first scene contrasts his 'brains and integrity' against a lumbering and ungainly Gorlopis:

Keyes:

> Now look Gorlopis. Every month hundreds of
> claims come to this desk. Some of them are
> phonies and I know which ones. How do I know?
> Because my little man tells me.

Gorlopis:

> What little man?

Keyes:

> The little man in here. (He gestures towards
> his chest.) Every time one of these phonies
> comes along he ties knots in my stomach, I
> can't eat. Yours was one of them ...

This rather humorous exchange establishes Keyes's investigative zeal from the start. He will clearly be crucial to plot development as his persistent acumen and intuition acts as the principal obstacle to the success of their fraudulent plans. He is a loyal if reluctant servant of the system, dismayed by a company which will 'write anything down just to get it on the sales sheet'. His know-how is brilliantly displayed in the scene where he allows Norton to 'run with the ball' and ultimately make a hash of his meeting with Phyllis. Norton's executive position has been acquired through privilege and nepotism, which itself is a tale role relevant to the narrative as he represents a refutation of the American Dream of success through a competitive meritocracy. The following exchange captures the contrast between the priggish Norton and the astute Keyes:

Norton:

> I was raised in the insurance business, Mr Keyes.

Keyes:

> Yeah. In the front office. Come now, you've never read an actuarial table in your life, have you? Why, they've got ten volumes on suicide alone. Suicide by race, by color, by occupation ... Suicide by poison, subdivided by types of poison, such as corrosive, irritant, systemic, gaseous, narcotic, alkaloid, protein and so forth. Suicide by leaps, subdivided by leaps from high places, under wheels of trains, under wheels of trucks, under the feet of horses, from steamboats. But Mr Norton, of all the cases on record, there is not one single case of suicide by leap from the rear end of a moving train.

The sheer linguistic density of this list, delivered by memory, is enough to silence Norton and assert Keyes's authority.

> the only conventional 'marriage' in the film

Keyes may have the brains and integrity but he remains a rather isolated figure. He has a mistrust of all women and indeed of all those who work in the insurance business. Since a sustained relationship with a partner is often denied to men in film noir, his only rote to friendship is through the buddy system with Neff. Wilder and a range of critics have pointed to the Neff-Keyes relationship as the only conventional 'marriage' in the film and we have already seen this in the analysis of the ending. If we continue the analogy of marriage, then the proposal must come when Keyes invites Neff to become his assistant and lyrically espouses the value of a claims man:

Keyes:

> To me a claims man is a surgeon, that desk is
> an operating table, and those pencils are
> scalpels and bone chisels. And these papers
> are not just forms and statistics and claims
> for compensation. They're alive. They're
> packed with drama, with twisted hopes and
> crooked dreams. A claims man, Walter, is a
> doctor and a bloodhound ... and a cop and a
> judge and a jury and a father confessor all in
> one.

Significantly this speech is delivered more or less simultaneously as Phyllis phones Walter to finalise their plans for murder, Wilder offering a sardonic contrast to Keyes's integrity. His offer is unrequited, leading him to conclude that Walter is 'not smarter' than the rest of the salesmen, 'just a little taller'.

MINOR CHARACTERS

A number of minor characters have contributions within the narrative through the significant tale roles they occupy. It is worth briefly alluding to their functions in the narrative.

Lola Lola acts as a major contrast to the femmes fatales. In Contexts: Generic classifications we will look in more detail at the generic depiction of women, but in general wives or mothers were seen as 'dull and insipid' a dutiful, conformist contrast to the femmes fatales. Lola may be moral and virtuous but even she goes against type. She is willing to go against her father in her secret rendezvous with the volatile Zachetti and she openly expresses dislike and suspicions of her stepmother. Along with Keyes, she develops into an important plot force in Act IV as her threat to implicate Phyllis in two murders is regarded by Neff as 'dynamite'. She also allows Neff the opportunity to expiate his sins and attempt some atonement in the friendship he offers her. Her revelation that she saw Phyllis in mourning dress before her father's death with eyes that had 'that look in them' provides information which unsettles Neff as he fades from actor to mere agent. Peter Evans summarised Lola as: 'a young woman blossoming naturally, despite all the odds into maturity, even if restricted by the virginal stereotype that all the nice boys in the audience were to go for once the initial excitement but ultimately castrating realities of the femme fatale had been worked out of their systems' (1994, p. 172).

Mr Dietrichson Mr Dietrichson represents everything Neff strives to avoid in his work and his relationships. Dour, boorish and exhausted, he is worn down by the economic burdens he carries as the provider, and it is a role he seems to carry reluctantly. His lines are delivered in mumbles and grunts and pleasure is something alien to his life. Even the reunion, a vain attempt to revisit the carefree days of youth, is something that he feels he cannot freely attend:

```
Phyllis:
        He was a Stanford man, Mr Neff. And he still
        goes to his class reunion every year.
Dietrichson:
        What's wrong with that? Can't I have a little
        fun even once a year?
```

His conversations with his wife and daughter are prohibitive, objecting to the former's spending and the latter's social arrangements. Ironically, his power is ultimately negated in both cases.

the threat of discovery which is subsequently delayed

Nino Zachetti An impetuous, rebellious adolescent, Zachetti contrasts strongly with the shrewd, cautious characters around him. His relationship with Phyllis is initially a surprise when he has formerly been attached to Lola, but his volatility makes him dangerously susceptible to the machinations of Phyllis.

Norton Norton, as we have seen, is principally present as a symbol of how even in the new country, old money and power retains positions of authority. However, a swipe is made at the old guard through Keyes's intellectual authority.

Mr Jackson Porter Hall fulfils a largely comic role as Jackson. As Keyes arrives closer to his solution, his comic presence undercuts the tension at the moment when Neff is almost discovered. As the only character who could genuinely place Neff on the train, Wilder plays with the threat of discovery in a film which continually thwarts our expectations. His questions to Neff ('Ever been in Oregon Mr Neff ... It's the name ... There's a family of Neffs in Corvalis') are more burlesque as they play with the threat of discovery which is subsequently delayed in the narrative. However, within the plot, his willingness to swear that the figure on the train was not Dietrichson is enough to substantiate Keyes's growing assuredness of fraud and murder.

Gorlopis If Norton is one extreme of the social scale, then Gorlopis is the other. He principally functions as a foil to Keyes so that Wilder can assert the rigour and authority of the latter from the start. He represents the ordinary man trying to secure modest gains from the system through minor acts of fraud.

style

mise-en-scène

Key elements of mise-en-scène include setting, lighting, costume, make-up and the positioning of characters and objects within a frame. Some of these have already been considered and some will be discussed later (see Contexts: Generic classifications) but it is worth analysing these categories now to see how they apply to *Double Indemnity*.

SETTING & PROPS

Richard Schickel commented on *Double Indemnity*:

> the movie has a very firm sense of place – no movie, documentary or fictional, offers a better sense of how the Los Angeles of its moment looked – but at the same time it energises that reality with a subtle air of menace. And few movies of any era have more deliciously proved the writerly adage that landscape is character. You could charge L.A. as a co-conspirator in the crimes this movie relates.
>
> *BFI Film Classics, 1992, p. 10*

Los Angeles had long been recognised as an alternative to some of the established northern American cities. Its climate and culture enabled it to retain some sense of a new frontier. The myth-making properties of the film industry added to its glamour. Many of its key industries such as film industry and real estate relied upon hype and bluster for their success, and perhaps Neff's insouciant forwardness is indicative of a regional psyche.

Wilder uses both the cityscape at the start of the film and images of decadent suburbia to capture this world. In addition, the Hollywood hills and a brief coastal car journey are included to capture its geographical scope in scenes between Neff and Lola. (This is in marked contrast to the claustrophobic settings in which Neff and Phyllis conduct their relationship.) Even its proximity to a foreign country, Mexico, is alluded to

consider what is absent, along with what is present

as the destination for Neff's escape – a world elsewhere he never quite reaches.

The Dietrichson House Neff describes the Dietrichson house as 'one of those California Spanish houses everyone was nuts about ten or fifteen years ago. This one must have cost somebody about 30,000 bucks, that is if he ever finished paying for it …' The fact that people 'were nuts' about these houses lends the impression that it is past its best, an inference given more weight in the interior shots.

Neff first arrives on a sunny May afternoon, with children playing on the road, overlooking the city below. The light exterior swiftly moves to a rather dark, stuffy interior. Neff comments, 'The living room was still stuffy from last night's cigars. The windows were closed and the sunshine coming in through the Venetian blinds showed up the dust in the air'. The lingering cigar smoke makes the audience subliminally aware of Dietrichson, an effect intensified by framed photographs of himself and Lola on the piano. With mise-en-scène we must consider what is absent, along with what is present, and it is noteworthy that no photograph of Phyllis is found, suggesting alienation from the family unit. (Remember her grievance that his life insurance all goes to his daughter, not Phyllis herself.) The furniture is 'corny and old-fashioned', more Dietrichson than Phyllis, indicating his frugal characteristics.

Neff's Apartment In the early 1930s, Billy Wilder roomed in a bachelor pad at the Chateau Marmont. For a short period, he roomed with the actor Peter Lorre, 'sharing Campbell's soup for dinner'. The transitory, impersonal feel is captured in Neff's apartment which lacks some of the more obvious signs of engagement with the space. The walls are largely unadorned bar a few framed boxing photographs and sporting prints, as well as a few sporting trophies which are presumably for football if his banter with Dietrichson is anything to go by. The furniture is plain and functional and there are no markers of family or friendship. When he goes to get Phyllis a drink only bourbon is available and there are no signs of food in the kitchen, as befits a bachelor who squeezes 'a grapefruit once in a while. Get the rest down at the corner drugstore'.

The room captures both Neff's lack of attachment and perhaps a sad isolation which he fills with his flirtations – which take such a serious diversion when he meets Phyllis.

The door to Neff's apartment merits a special mention as unusually and perhaps unnaturally it opens *outwards* onto the hallway. This provides some powerful visual opportunities. When Phyllis first visits, Schrader's trapezoids of light (see Lighting on p. 51) are in evidence as she appears framed in angular light, contrasting with the darkness within. Later, after the murder, the same door masks her in shadow as she hides behind it to avoid detection by Keyes, who has just visited Walter to share his latest hunch. This door has both dramatic and symbolic value, part of the semiology of light and dark and duplicity. Wilder has admitted it was a mistake for the door to open outwards and it is one of the few examples of style and expressionism overriding realism.

Insurance Company The Pacific All Risk Insurance Company occupies the entire eleventh and twelfth floors of the Pacific Building. The executive offices and claims and sales departments are on the twelfth floor and they all open onto a balcony which runs all the way around. The balcony provides views of the eleventh floor below, where one enormous room is filled with desks and desk lights and a range of bureaucratic accoutrements. Whilst it may not be Kafka-esque, the interminable rows of desks below do give an insight into the monotony of paperwork undertaken by the lower-middle-class clerics. It is significant in the opening segment that the wounded Neff pauses and looks down from this balcony with a wry smile, as his attempt to escape this conformity and predictability has so tragically backfired. The scenes of the night workers cleaning the office captures the relentless nature of economic activity and a sense of the social hierarchy. Most of the cleaning staff are black Americans, reflecting a racial and racist divide in the division of labour.

Office hierarchies are further evident later when we see the spacious interior of the company President, Edward S. Norton Jr. The very word Jr suggests nepotism, someone who has inherited, not earned, their position. Old family photographs, a carved American eagle and a fussily carved armchair are just some of the items which distinguish his environment from that of the others. The low-level chairs reserved for visitors provide another route for his power to be established.

Neff's office, like his apartment, is spartan and contains once again the eponymous Venetian blinds. It is significant that his confession in this most secular world is dictated through his dictaphone. This prop was one of the most subtle and effective changes from novel to screenplay. Neff and Keyes communicate too much through wit and banter for the sincerity of Neff's confession to be delivered face to face. This device is impersonal and provides a realistic context for the voice-over as we overhear Neff's address to another character, rather than the dramatic artifice of Neff addressing the viewer directly.

LIGHTING

As we will discover in considerations of genre, the distinct use of lighting (see Cinematic Terms: low-key lighting) is one of the distinctive features of film noir and one of the most significant stylistic traits of *Double Indemnity*. It was suggested that the prevailing atmosphere of darkness emphasised the underbelly of society, the tenebrous side of humanity reflected in this covert world.

The chiaroscuro effects resulting from low-key lighting are employed in *Double Indemnity* and are evident in the opening scene (see Narrative & Form: Opening) as the wounded Neff makes his way to his office to begin his confession. The opening external shots show the dark city streets illuminated by street lamps and the neon sign of the Pacific Building. As Neff enters, his darkened, halting figure becomes a partial incarnation of the portentous shadow prefaced in the opening credits. In the foyer, the only light is the rhomboid emanating from the elevator at obtuse angles. As he enters his office, the main light enters from the blinds, symbolically the source of light emanating from elsewhere. As he sits, a desk light provides the central light source, providing chiaroscuro illumination of the face. Neff speaks, his hat still on, and this provides further shadowing effects for his face. His face is centre frame in close up, but a distinctive shadow from a filing cabinet occupies considerable space, reminding us of 'a space that is continually cut into ribbons of light'

the world of shadows inhabited by the central characters. Paul Schrader has shown how:

> Light enters the dingy rooms of film noir in such odd shapes – jagged trapezoids, obtuse triangles, vertical slits – that one suspects the windows were cut out with a penknife. No character can speak authoritatively from a space that is continually cut into ribbons of light.
>
> *1972, p. 11*

This context certainly informs Neff's wavering confession and captures the prevailing mood of fatalism.

Some of the symbolic and technical features of lighting are found in Neff's first meeting with Phyllis. He drives to the Dietrichson household on a sunny afternoon in late May, providing us with one of the few images of a sun-drenched Los Angeles. Wilder quickly moves action to the inside of the Dietrichson house where lighting is restricted and once again the blinds diffuse the external brightness. He was extremely fortunate in his choice of John Seitz as cameraman, who used finely ground aluminium filings to reflect sunlight from the windows, creating the dusty effect in the Dietrichson living room suggesting a house past its best. In one of the first classic shots, Phyllis sits cross-legged on the armchair, the shadows partially resting across her chest and face, but her legs, accentuated by the anklet and the pompoms on her shoes are illuminated in clear light, beginning the fetishisation of the femme fatale. It is significant that as she gets Neff to elucidate upon his insurance portfolio, leading to the first tentative broaching of accident insurance, a distinct shadow is cast on the living room wall, strangely indicative of her ulterior motive.

One of the most distinctive and possibly archetypal uses of lighting in the film occurs when Phyllis first visits Neff's apartment. Significantly, the now obsessed Neff stands in his darkened room, the dark encoding his mood of fatalism. The only light initially comes from the external street lights, and the mordant feel is accentuated by the rain falling outside. As he opens the door (outwards) to Phyllis, once again light enters from the external environment of the apartment corridor. When Phyllis enters, Neff

'I tried for a very realistic picture'

switches the lights on but the mezzo light seems to reduce the filler light to create a harsher sense of realism. Wilder described the scene in the following way:

> There was some *dramatic* lighting, yes, but it was newsreel lighting. That was the ideal. I'm not saying that every shot was a masterpiece, but sometimes even in newsreel you get a masterpiece shot. That was the approach. No phony setups ... We used a little mezzo light in the apartment when Stanwyck comes to see MacMurray in the apartment – this is when he makes up his mind to commit murder.
>
> *Conversations with Wilder, 1999, p. 53*

The most absorbing scene of darkness occurs in the kitchen where Neff goes to mix the bourbon. The two are encased in almost complete darkness – even the refrigerator fails to shed any light! The only true light is reflected in Phyllis's eyes, particularly as she comments 'perhaps it was worth it' on the women who risked death in their desperate attempts to rid themselves of their husbands. As they return and sit in the living room, Phyllis is never fully illuminated. Rather, the side lamp keeps half her face in the shade and there is avoidance of conventional, romantic lighting.

Some critics see strong links between the visual style of *Double Indemnity* and the lighting and framing techniques of German expressionism. Wilder himself has drawn links between the visual style of *Double Indemnity* and films which had grown *out of* the German expressionist movement (although he denies a specific link with the movement itself):

> We had to be realistic. You had to believe the situation and the characters, or all was lost. I insisted on black and white, of course, and in making operettas I'd learned that sometimes one technical shot destroyed a picture. You could say that *Double Indemnity* was based on the principle of *M* [Fritz Lang, 1931], the very good picture starring Peter Lorre. I had a feeling, something in my head, *M* was on my mind. I tried for a very realistic picture – a few little tricks, but not very tricky. *M* was the look of the picture. It was a

picture that looked like a newsreel. You never realise it was staged. But like a newsreel, you look to grab a moment of truth, and exploit it.

Conversations with Wilder, 1999, p. 53

The murder scene itself takes place at night and the darkness of the car is illuminated only by the oncoming traffic. The body is dumped on the tracks in the dark and Neff and Phyllis exchange their final kiss in half-shadow. As Neff makes his nervous, covert entrance back to his apartment, an ominous shadow follows him up the stairs.

Against the ominous, night for day, lighting, the representation of Lola through lighting emphasises her innocence and moral decency. Scenes with Lola take place very much in the more normalised world where filler light is used to soften some of the extremes of character and situation. She is often illuminated by the 'even, flat, high–key lighting' described by Janey Place (1998) as typical of the 'nurturing woman' who occupies a safer world. Montage sequences between Lola and Neff on their coastal drive or laughing in a restaurant have a more naturalistic emphasis. Their friendship is not conducted covertly in darkness and even their night-time scene on the hill overlooking the Hollywood bowl is effectively lit in the background by a romantic image reinforced by the music.

The penultimate scene of the film provides one of the starkest uses of darkness and one entirely appropriate to the mood. Before Neff arrives, Phyllis turns off the lights, enveloping the room in darkness. As they both double-cross one another, Neff intensifies the atmosphere by drawing the blinds *and* drawing the curtains to hide their actions from view. If Neff achieves some redemptive effects in his scenes with Lola, then Phyllis seems to seek this after she has shot Walter and uncharacteristic sentiment grips her. Wilder illuminates her with more top lighting to create a more conventional romantic image, and here she may even temporarily occupy the softer tones of the nurturing woman. Yet typical of the film's contrapuntal movement and Wilder's heightened sense of irony, this moment is shattered as her eyes register the gun at her side, prior to Neff's shooting of her and her final return to the shadows.

Reassertion of
the patriarchy

COSTUME, HAIR & MAKE-UP

Barbara Stanwyck's costume as Phyllis is most noticeable as it carries the iconography of the femme fatale. From her first entrance, clad only in her towel, her sexuality is foregrounded. When she enters the room, she is still buttoning her dress, implying a lack of propriety. As she sits cross-legged the combination of the ludicrous pompoms and the anklet draws Neff and the audience's attention to her legs. (This exemplifies what many feminists have described as the assumption that the viewer is male.)

Wilder wondered whether the blonde wig was a step too far:

> I questioned the wig, but it was proper, because it was a phony wig. It was an obviously phony wig. And the anklet – the equipment of a woman, you know, that is married to this kind of man. They scream for murder.
>
> *Conversations with Wilder, 1999, p. 48*

In her visit to Neff's apartment, Phyllis's liberated, independent qualities are signified through dress, particularly the trousers she wears. The contrast between her black trousers and white blouse embody quintessential noir sensibilities and complement the stark mood of the scene. The emphasis on sexuality is retained through the tight, transparent sweater.

Some of the semantics of dress can be best seen when Neff first meets Dietrichson to gain his unknowing signature on the accident insurance policy. Neff wears his usual lightly shaded suit, but looks slightly more officious in a plain white shirt compared to the slightly lined shirts he has previously sported. Against his sharp, dapper appearance, Dietrichson lies exhausted, unkempt on the sofa. His tie is removed, his top button unbuttoned, as he barely raises the energy to affix his signature to the policy. His trudging walk and hunched deportment contrast powerfully with Neff's purposeful stride. The responsibilities of work, routine and responsibility appear to have worn him down and the contrast between himself and Neff makes Phyllis's motivation all the more comprehensible.

In this scene, we also have a telling contrast between femme fatale and 'nurturing woman'. In her short-sleeve blouse buttoned to the neck and her calf-length skirt, Lola is an image of propriety, although her subsequent

Phyllis, as black widow, and
Neff in officious white shirt,
talk of 'double indemnity'

rebellion belies her prim appearance. Phyllis is perhaps more obviously the black widow here than in any other scene. She wears a black dress, the skirt of which consists of numerous tassels which she flirtatiously plays with as the signature is written, a motif for the ensnaring taking place. The elaborate dress, expensive brooch and refocus on her legs once again emphasise her sexuality. She is as unmaternal as could be imagined, making the juxtaposition with her stepdaughter all the more striking. Dietrichson's frugality seems to find its chief target in the flamboyance of his wife's clothing and spending: 'Who needs a hat in California?'

Phyllis appears more conventionally as expected, in her secret supermarket liaisons with Neff. (It is worth considering the effect of these full shelves on a war-torn, rationed Europe. Even here, the myth and reality of the new superpower were being signified.) Yet, in their final meeting, as Keyes's investigations burden them further, her duplicity is captured through the sunglasses she wears indoors. As Neff fails to persuade to stop her claiming, she removes the sunglasses to fix him with an icy stare to underscore the force of her threat to frame him, should he try to wriggle out now. In her final appearance, the flowing silken house pyjamas provide an image of flowing sensuality and we return to the iconography of the lit cigarette as she contemptuously listens to his attempts to achieve the final double-cross. The feminine appearance contradicts the mettle of her actions: the gun which shoots Neff is hidden in a silk scarf beneath the sofa. Whilst Phyllis is presented in a stylish, fetishised manner, her depiction lacks the rather gothic and macabre excess of Cain's novel. Phyllis behaves with utter conviction as she appears before Norton in her mourning dress and Neff compliments her on her performance. Wilder's wish for authenticity and realism dominates at all times.

Other uses of costume remain important in the film. Neff appears generally in light suits with high-waisted trousers, emphasising his height and masculine build. In the Pacific Building, he is often seen wearing his hat indoors, a subtle swipe at formality which typifies some of his actions. It is significant that the hat is removed before his meeting with Norton and out of respect for Lola after her father's murder. His switch to a conservative navy blue suit to imitate Dietrichson is the only occasion we see him in such sober tones, and these darker tones ominously reflect his purpose.

Barton Keyes, from his first appearance, sleeves partially rolled, waistcoat pockets bulging with pens, papers and tables, is every inch the persistent and purposeful claims investigator. His rejection of formal niceties is marvellously captured in his exchange with the priggish Norton prior to the latter's unsuccessful interrogation of Phyllis. As he enters Norton's office, he is chastised for failure to wear his jacket. Norton, on the other hand, wears a three-piece suit, embellished by a carnation in his lapel and a handkerchief neatly folded in his top pocket. Clothing becomes a metaphor for the differences between them as Norton's formal, stilted, questioning backfires, leaving Phyllis in the ascendant, something Keyes's dogged acumen would never have allowed. As Keyes leaves the office, having downed a glass of water in one and splashed water without concern over his tie and waistcoat, he sardonically states, 'next time I'll rent a tuxedo'.

Minor characters also transmit messages through their dress. Gorlopis, with his shirt stained with sweat and oil, symbolises the lower orders trying to get ahead through a minor and obvious insurance scam. Jackson should represent a telling threat to Neff but somehow that wide-rimmed, Stetson hat reduces him to comic caricature, a rural hickster out of place in this quick, cosmopolitan city, who is unable to identify the suspect right under his nose. Zachetti is rarely seen but as he waits for Lola his half-mast, baggy, pleated trousers and white socks capture elements of his youth.

sound

Wilder has said that the score for a film should be 'invisible' – that its ability to accentuate and punctuate a film should occur at a subconscious level, emphasising moods without us being aware. Reference has already been made to the portentous, gloomy qualities of the score by Miklos Rozsa, who was one of Wilder's favourite composers. The music sets the tone powerfully with its strident tones in the opening credits.

match the increasingly tragic turn of events

The music generally functions as parallel sound. When Neff makes his first two journeys to the Dietrichson house, the music has a more romantic, almost pastoral tone. As Phyllis makes her first appearance in the towel and Neff makes his rather corny joke, 'I'd hate to think of your having a smashed fender or something while you're not, fully covered', his innuendo is underlined by a rather playful flute. The romantic music later disappears after Neff becomes aware of Phyllis's plans and Rozsa's harsh refrain is increasingly deployed in different variations and tempos to match the increasingly tragic turn of events. Climactic strings are used to capture the tension of Dietrichson's murder which takes place off screen.

Contrapuntal sound is used more sparingly in the film. One of the most powerful examples occurs in the penultimate scene, immediately after Phyllis has shot Neff. Her apparent sentiment and regret is captured in the return of the more romantic, pastoral music which characterised their earlier exchanges. However, as the music builds and they embrace for the final time, Phyllis suddenly feels the gun and her expression changes to shock. At this point, the music ceases immediately and two loud shots resonate, followed by silence and stillness. The music has lulled the audience into false security, wrongly signalling a romantic dénouement before a brutal realism reinforces itself through the diegetic sound of the gun.

BRIDGING MUSIC

The continuity of the film is assisted by the subtle use of bridging music. It often accompanies the switch from scene to a montage sequence. The ominous tones of Rozsa's score can be heard as Neff leaves Dietrichson's house after becoming aware of Phyllis's plans to kill her husband and it accompanies the sequence from the drive-in back to his apartment where its foreboding qualities increase before Phyllis's arrival at the apartment. It is also used subtly in the sequence which illustrates Neff's construction of alibis as he asks Charlie to wash his car, rings a colleague, changes his suit and leaves cards in appropriate places to check no one has called round or rung.

DIEGETIC AND NON-DIEGETIC SOUND

Most sound in the film is diegetic, integral to the action in the scene, with the music functioning as the main non-diegetic support. Neff's voice-overs have already been discussed in considerations of narrative but it is unusual that they have both diegetic and non-diegetic qualities. His confession to Keyes takes place in the present diegetically but the switch to the past through dissolve and bridging music subtly gives the voice-over non-diegetic qualities as it contextualises the events we are about to see. In montage sequences, the voice-over is more conventional and exclusively non-diegetic in its operation.

editing

The function of editing has largely been discussed under considerations of narrative. However it is worth re-emphasising the effects of continuity editing in maintaining the illusion of naturalism. The shot/reverse shot technique was extremely common in the 1940s and Wilder deployed it to good effect in *Double Indemnity*.

We will look at aspects of editing in the scene where Neff goes to the Dietrichson house to gain Mr Dietrichson's signature. While analysing the scene, it is also worth considering aspects of framing and focus. The scene begins with an establishing shot, where the camera pans back from Lola and Phyllis playing checkers, to Dietrichson lying on the sofa, to Neff sitting on the armchair in the foreground. This apparently stable mise-en-scène is quickly fragmented through dialogue, costume and telling character contrast (see Costume, hair and make-up on p. 56).

The first close-up is of Dietrichson, who doesn't even move to deliver his complaint that Phyllis wastes his money; an arch of the head simply captures his indolence. He then establishes an eyeline gaze that cuts us back to Neff, espousing the value of accident insurance. Neff's close-up is framed by the lamp on the left and the fireplace on the right. Their dialogue continues as the camera cuts back to Dietrichson wearily cutting the sales pitch.

editing

binds the narrative and captures character

The camera cuts back to Lola and Phyllis as the family unity is further shattered by Lola's assertion that checkers is boring. A further cut back to include all four characters places Lola in the centre, framed by the rest of the characters. Phyllis's deliberately inflammatory reference to Lola's possible liaison with Zachetti prompts a cut to a close-up of Dietrichson, as he attempts to assert his paternal authority. A shot/reverse shot pattern is again established through the close-up on Lola as she replies in an assertive manner. The camera cuts back to frame all four characters, before a further cut follows her confident walk from the room.

Lola's exit effects a significant alteration to character positioning and framing. Phyllis moves to the foreground, Neff moves to the sofa and Dietrichson is now in the centre, ensnared by those around him. A cut to film his signature from behind with Phyllis looking on in the distance subtly reflects her eagerness. As the signature is written, we receive a significant close-up of Neff and his conspiratorial gaze towards Phyllis. These edits are reinforced by the reintroduction of Rozsa's theme. The reverse shot allows her to return the gaze and their feelings are expressed without any dialogue. A close-up to Neff takes them from this private, unspoken exchange and a shot of all three shows that business is concluded. As they leave the room, a camera in mid-shot follows them from hallway to living room and as they reach the hallway an omniscient perspective from living room to hallway shows Neff leaving and Dietrichson climbing the stairs.

Once outside, a mid-shot frames Phyllis and Neff. As he mentions the 'double indemnity' for the first time, the camera cuts to close-up and the reversal shot close-up of Phyllis captures her savouring his words and contemplating the further gains she could make.

Continuity editing almost seamlessly binds the narrative and captures character perspective and viewpoint.

contexts

cultural & ideological

Classic film noir is said to have begun major production with *The Maltese Falcon* in 1941 and ended with *Touch of Evil* in 1958. *Double Indemnity* was produced at a transitional time for this expanding genre and by the end of the decade the number in production had risen from four in 1942 to twenty-nine by 1947.

The term film noir derives from a French literary source. The 'Roman noir' was the name give to popular types of low-life fiction depicting crime and corruption. Writers such as James M. Cain were having their work translated into trashy French crime magazines. These novels and stories, largely of the 1930s, were to inform the American cinema of the 1940s and 1950s. Richard Schickel points out that: 'the first public use of the term (film noir) appears to have been in a French film journal in 1946 and it did not become common American critical coinage for at least another twenty five years. By 1946, French critics seeing the American films they had missed during the war, noticed the new mood of "cynicism, pessimism and darkness" that had crept into American cinema' (1992, p. 12).

POST-WAR DISILLUSIONMENT

Although *Double Indemnity* was produced before the end of the war, it tapped into a mood of disillusionment that was growing in America. In his excellent essay on film noir, the screenwriter and director Paul Schrader traces how the 'downer' that hit the US after the war was a delayed reaction to the 1930s. Movies had raised public spirits during the depression and the darker mood that surfaced towards the end of the decade was snuffed out by the patriotic fervour of the Second World War. Schrader writes:

> The unflinching noir vision of *Double Indemnity* came as a shock in 1944, and the film was almost blocked by the combined efforts of

a mood of cynicism and claustrophobia

Paramount, the Hays Office, and star Fred MacMurray. Three years later, however, *Double Indemnity*s were dropping off the studio assembly lines.

1972, p. 12

A mood of post-war gloom led to a halting of idealistic notions of American identity. The Westerns of the 1930s had celebrated the frontier spirit and the sense of opportunity and space offered by this new nation. Noir replaced this with a mood of cynicism and claustrophobia; tangible darkness invaded space creating doubt and paranoia. America had promised success through industriousness and endeavour and yet for many this was unattainable. If paths were blocked then individuals turned to crime and violence. Economically, Walter Neff no longer wishes to be the servant of the insurance system he has served all his years. He believes he has the intelligence and the know-how to subvert the system. In one of his most significant monologues Neff confesses through the office dictaphone to Keyes:

```
Because it was all tied up with something I
had been thinking about for years, since long
before I ever ran into Phyllis Dietrichson.
Because - you know how it is Keyes? In this
business you can't sleep for trying to figure
out all the tricks they could pull on you.
You're like the guy behind the roulette wheel,
watching the customers to make sure they don't
crook the house. And then one night, you get
to thinking how you could crook the house
yourself. And do it smart. Because you've got
that wheel right under your hands. You know
every notch in it by heart. And you figure all
you need is a plant out front, a shill to put
down the bet. And suddenly the doorbell rings
and the whole set up is right there in the
room with you ...
```

reversal of the conventional moral order

Criminals were actually sensationalised during this period. Gangsters had broken the oppressive and paternalistic rules of society to gain wealth and power and in some cases achieved the status of anti-heroes. This reversal of the conventional moral order had a clear influence on the predominant sensibilities of *Double Indemnity*.

The cohesive view of society which war-time cinema had tried to promote was being challenged by the fragmented world that individuals actually confronted. 'The disillusionment that many soldiers, small businessmen, and housewife/factory employees felt in returning to a peacetime economy was directly mirrored in the sordidness of the urban crime film' (Paul Schrader, 1972, pp. 9–10). In 'Underworld USA', Colin McArthur speculates that the consequences of the Depression, the Second World War and eventually the Cold War led to a general mood of uncertainty, 'paralleled in the general mood of malaise, the loneliness, and angst and the lack of clarity about the characters' motives in the thrillers' (*The Cinema Book*, 1999, p. 186). Men were threatened by the work of women in industry during the war and felt undermined by their new independence. Men's need to dominate and control once more introduced a new element of misogyny which will be analysed now under Generic classifications. Ideals of marital loyalty were undermined by portrayals of infidelity and mistrust in films such as *The Blue Dahlia* (which Chandler scripted after *Double Indemnity*) and *The Best Years of Our Lives*.

generic classifications

Precise definitions of film noir prove elusive as considerable debate exists between those who identify recurrent precise generic conventions and those who see more subtle qualities of style and tone which pervade the noir movement. Paul Schrader agrees with Robert Durgant's assertion that film noir is not in the strictest of terms a genre: 'It is not defined, as are the western and gangster genres, by conventions of setting and conflict but rather by the more subtle qualities of tone and mood' (1972, p. 2). Janey Place continued this viewpoint when she claimed that 'unlike genres, defined by objects and subjects, but like other film movements, film noir is characterised by a remarkable homogeneous visual style with which it cuts

'different motion pictures with one cohesive visual style'

across genres' (*The Cinema Book*, 1999, p. 185). As Pam Cook points out, some critics disdain the use of the term 'movement' as it implies the films shared a political or aesthetic unity which their production histories cannot support. Movements such as Italian neo-realism were borne out of a precise political philosophy which bound the work together. The ties which bound film noir were less specific but ultimately more pervasive. Silver and Ward, who completed one of the lengthiest encyclopaedias of film noir, undertook research that took a random sample of seven film noirs to discover that 'different directors and cinematographers of great and small technical reputations, working at seven different studios, completed seven ostensibly different motion pictures with one cohesive visual style' (*The Cinema Book*, 1999, p. 184).

It is those elements of the 'cohesive visual style' which we will try to focus upon in our considerations of genre.

STYLISTICS

In a seminal essay on noir, Paul Schrader (1972, p. 11) posits seven features which provide an embryonic stylistic measure of some of the recurrent features of film noir:

1 The majority of the scenes are lit for night.

2 Oblique and vertical lines are preferred to horizontal. 'Obliquity adheres to the choreography of the city ... Oblique lines tend to splinter a screen, making it restless and unstable'.

3 The actors and the setting are given equal lighting emphasis. This can foreground the environment and make characters and their endeavours seem inconsequential. Richard Schickel writes how Los Angeles is so vividly realised in *Double Indemnity* that it almost acts as a key character in the film.

4 Compositional tension is preferred to physical action. The cinematography moves 'around' the actor rather than his physical action dictating the pace of events.

5 There is a Freudian attachment to water. As Neff looks out of his apartment, the 'sunny' Los Angeles glistens with rain.

'the how is always more important than the what'

6 There is a tendency for romantic narration. The 'narrator creates a mood of temps perdu: an irretrievable past, a predetermined fate, and an all-enveloping hopelessness. The dominant mood of fatalism is one of the strongest features of *Double Indemnity* and one which has been apparent in sections on narrative and character'.

7 A complex chronological order is frequently used. This can contribute to the sense of hopelessness as the extended flashbacks of *Double Indemnity* show us that fate has already run its course. Schrader claims the key noir principle was 'the how is always more important than the what'. In *Double Indemnity*, Neff's confession in the opening scene provides us with the what. It is the how which engages the audience and Keyes.

Many of the features which Schrader here identifies are indeed prevalent in film noir and we can discern many of them so clearly in *Double Indemnity*. Schrader's observations were developed by Place and Peterson in 'Some visual motifs of film noir'. They too emphasised the significance of the prevalent use of low-key lighting which 'opposes light and darkness, hiding faces, rooms and urban landscapes – and by extension, motivation and true character – in shadow and darkness' (*The Cinema Book*, 1999, p. 185). Allusion is also made to the distinctive framing devices which isolated characters and had alienating effects. They too refer to the oblique shadows which disorientate character and setting and create moods of uncertainty. There is enough here to suggest a similarity of style across the range of film noir and to confirm that the stylistic similarities were strong enough to constitute generic attributes.

THEMES

Whilst Schrader favours the notion of film noir as a movement, he can identify pervasive themes co-existing across film noir which often weave their way into the narrative structure. He cites Robert Durgnat's article, *The Family Tree of Film Noir* (August 1970), which divided film noir into eleven thematic categories. Headings such as Black Widow, Killers On The Run, Doppelgangers, Psychopaths and Middle-Class Murder were created. *Double Indemnity* is located in the 'Middle-Class Murder' section,

'a fear of the future'

under the sub-heading of the 'Corruption of the Not-So-Innocent-Male' (Interestingly, along with Cain's other classic, *The Postman Always Rings Twice*).

Schrader argues that each of Durgnat's themes sees a reversal of the previous order: 'The small time gangster has made it big and sits in the mayor's chair, the private eye has quit the police force in disgust, and the young heroine, sick of going along for the ride, is taking others for a ride' (1972, p. 11).

However, Schrader claims the dominant noir theme is a 'passion for the past and present, but also a fear of the future' (1972, p. 11). In *Double Indemnity* we only have past and a limited present. Neff's confession and the inevitability of capture and death leave him without a future. Much of Neff's actions in the second half of the film stem from his fear of the future, a fear which Phyllis does not seem to share.

The Femme Fatale and Women in Film Noir

In her seminal essay on *Women in Film Noir*, Janey Place (1998) identified eight stylistic and iconographical motifs (pp. 64–7) associated with the representation of women in film noir.

1 The iconography is explicitly sexual with long hair (blonde or dark), make up and jewellery.

2 Cigarettes have sexual connotations of liberation and phallic power.

3 'Dress – or the lack of it – defines the women.'

4 'Iconography of violence is a specific symbol of her unnatural phallic power.'

5 Framed portrait of women is a common motif.

6 Murders indicate narcissism or duplicity.

7 Women are generally centre frame or drawing our attention by focusing on the foreground.

8 Visual style expresses mood through darkness, both real in underlit and night-time scenes, and psychologically through shadow and claustrophobic settings which overwhelm the character.

generic classifications

Like Schrader, Place perceived patterns of representation which were prevalent across a range of films. She felt the femme fatale was a male fantasy and that ultimately the assertive woman is punished for the threat she posed to the patriarchal order. However she felt film noir 'gives us one of the few periods of film in which women are active, not static symbols, are intelligent and powerful, if destructively so, and derive power, not weakness from their sexuality' (*Women in Film Noir*, 1998, p. 47). As we have seen, we may not morally identify with Phyllis Dietrichson but we do marvel at her manipulative skill and the coolness she displays.

The male fear of women reached a peak towards the end of the Second World War. Women had successfully taken on traditional male jobs in the workplace and had worked with considerable success. Myths that they were incapable of certain aspects of economic production had been disproved and men felt uneasy as a result: 'the industrial world was shocked – and occasionally dismayed – that women, now 36% of the labor force, worked harder than men, required less supervision, had fewer industrial accidents, and did less damage to tools' (Marjorie Rosen, *Dark Cinema*, 1984, pp. 203–4). This economic and industrial success led to a desire for economic power and social engagement which transcended previous roles. Femmes fatales have ambitions which go beyond those usually allowed by the patriarchal system: 'She wants to be the owner of her own night club, not the owner's wife (*Night and the City*). She wants to be the star, not a recluse (*Sunset Boulevard*). She wants her husband's insurance money, not her comfortable middle class life (*Double Indemnity*)' (Janey Place, *Women in Film Noir*, 1998, p. 56).

This social liberation is mirrored by the sexual liberation of women in film noir. But if the working woman was forced to resume domestic duties after the war, then the sexually assertive woman was similarly punished for challenging the patriarchy in film noir. Behind the apparent liberated sexuality of the femmes fatales lies the misogynist force of the patriarchal order:

> ... the male protagonist in the film is usually alienated from his environment and one of the principal factors behind this alienation is the fact that the femme fatale is in possession of her own

> sexuality ... the femme fatale must be punished for this attempt at independence, usually by her death, thus restoring the balance of the patriarchal system.
>
> *John Tuska, 1984, p. 199*

If the femme fatale was one extreme of film noir, then the nurturing woman was the other. The nurturing woman was often a countervailing force and in *Double Indemnity* it is Lola who reignites Neff's conscience and forces him to reappraise his actions in his later bid for redemption. John Tuska saw 'two basic types of women in film noir ... the femmes fatales and the loving wives and mothers' (or daughters in *Double Indemnity*!). 'The femmes fatales are interesting, intelligent and often powerful, whereas the wives and mothers are dull and insipid' (1984, p. 202). At least Wilder's more complex direction does not quite make Lola as predictable as this but she clearly has more conformist tendencies.

Janey Place described the noir wife/mother as a 'nurturing woman' who 'in order to offer this alternative landscape of film noir, she herself must not be part of it' (1998, p. 60). We have already seen how Lola does not occupy the world of shadows and darkness inhabited by Neff and Phyllis. When Neff shares scenes with Lola, lighting tones appear to employ more filler light to reduce some of the more dramatic contrasts which typify his scenes with Phyllis (see Style: Lighting).

Representation of Men in Film Noir

If the archetypal female roles in film noir have been critically documented by feminist criticism, then John Tuska sees similar predetermined roles for men:

> Patriarchy is a double-edged sword. For men, it prescribes that they must perform in order to be loved, and part of performance must include subscribing to the success ethic. Keeping women in their 'place' means for men that they, too, must keep their place: they must go it alone with only the buddy system to sustain them; they cannot show too much emotion; above all they must find the meaning of life in activity, never contemplation.
>
> *1984, p. 215*

generic classifications

He argued that the roles of men are just as predetermined as those of women:

> It is their purpose in life to work, to provide, to protect, and to serve without ever questioning in the preservation of the way of life of their culture and their government. They never have a genuine and sustained relationship with a woman.

Barton Keyes fits many of the descriptions above as he is 'married' to his job with a sceptical approach towards relationships. His one flirtation with marriage was halted by the internal workings of his 'little man' who prompted an investigation of the woman he intended to marry, after which he discovered:

```
Keyes:

    And the stuff that came out. She'd been dyeing
    her hair ever since she was sixteen ... And as
    for her brother ...

Neff:

    I get the general idea. She was a tramp from a
    long line of tramps.
```

When Neff turns down the chance to work as Assistant Claims Investigator, whilst apparently dallying with 'Margie' on the telephone, Keyes looks upon him with disappointment. According to Keyes, Neff 'was just a shade less dumb than the rest of the outfit'. Indeed, critics have pointed out that Keyes's only committed relationship is his one with Neff, which Schickel describes as the only true husband and wife relationship in the film.

In contrast, as the anti-hero, Neff attempts to beat the system which he has subscribed to throughout his working life and as a result the system wins and takes his life. The noir hero is often a loner, without the established systems of family or supportive friendships. At one point Phyllis expresses envy at the isolated quality of Neff's existence which seems to embody the very freedoms she desires:

difficult to secure approval from the Breen Office

Phyllis:

> It's nice here Walter. Who takes care of it
> for you?

Neff:

> Coloured woman comes in a couple of times a
> week.

Phyllis:

> Cook your own breakfast?

Neff:

> Squeeze a grapefruit once in a while. Get the
> rest down at the corner drugstore.

Phyllis:

> Sounds wonderful. Just strangers beside you.
> You don't know them and you don't hate them.

Neff is initially happy in his detachment but towards the end of the film, he seems to seek escape and even redemption from his isolated existence in his paternalistic relationship with Lola.

production history

SCREENPLAY

Most of our knowledge of the production history of *Double Indemnity* is focused on pre-production and in particular the contentious evolution of the screenplay. The success of Cain's novels produced great excitement in Hollywood. *The Postman Always Rings Twice* was critically acclaimed and a bestseller. When *Double Indemnity* was later serialised in *Liberty* magazine it was claimed that it increased the magazine's circulation to eight million copies.

However, enthusiasm for the rights to the novels was tempered by the realisation that it would be very difficult to secure approval from the Breen Office due to their sexual content and particularly because of their moral ambivalence. Adaptations would have to be so sanitised that they would lose the very elements which excited movie producers. Richard Schickel

production history

shows how the interference of the Breen Office caused Columbia to drop out of the bidding and eventually halved the value from $50,000 to the $25,000 MGM finally paid. Similar pressures were brought to bear on the bidding for *Double Indemnity* where a proposed figure of $25,000 was reduced to the $15,000 Paramount paid, a modest amount for such a hot property.

Wilder was so enthused by the novel that he finished it in fifty-eight minutes – considerably quicker that the two hours, fifty minutes and seven seconds recommended reading time given in *Liberty* magazine where the novel was first serialised.

Wilder presumed the script would be another collaboration with Charles Bracket, with whom he had first collaborated in 1938.

However when the conservative Bracket read the novel, he condemned it unequivocally as 'disgusting' and refused any possible collaboration. Arguments ensued, but Bracket would not even contemplate working on a film which he found so morally reprehensible. Joseph Sistrom, upon Wilder's suggestion, then asked Cain for support, but he was already writing another screenplay for 20th Century Fox. Joseph Sistrom, Associate Producer on *Double Indemnity*, then suggested Raymond Chandler, whom he felt belonged to a similar noir tradition, and Wilder, as we have seen, was greatly impressed by the quality of Chandler's writing. Yet in 1943, Chandler had written to his publisher, Alfred Knopf, complaining of the links critics made between his own prose and the hard-boiled tradition of Hammet and Cain. He described Cain in the following manner:

> Everything he touches smells like a billy goat. He is every kind of writer I detest, a faux naif, a Proust in greasy overalls, a dirty little boy with a piece of chalk and a board fence and nobody looking. Such people are the offal of literature, not because they write about dirty things but because they do it in a dirty way.

The letter did not bode well for the collaboration but Chandler was relieved to get the post, partly because of the modest payments he received from his publisher. In his first meeting with Sistrom and Wilder, they were taken aback by the modesty of his terms. He requested $150 a week whilst

Chandler found Wilder very difficult

writing, which he thought would take approximately a month. Sistrom subsequently informed him that he would be paid $750 a week for as long as the script took to write and he would also receive an office in the writer's building and a secretary.

Wilder was keen to work with Chandler whom he once described to John Tuska as 'a naïve, sweet, warm man'. The differences between them were pronounced as many have documented. Richard Schickel described Wilder as 'small, sharp faced, casually dressed, looking energetic and eager ... dwarfed by the older, tweedy, ponderous Chandler, who was, we know, a shy and solitary man, in contrast to the gregarious Wilder' (1992, p. 35).

Chandler found Wilder very difficult to work with. Wilder paced the room, often using a malacca cane to emphasise a point. He offended Chandler's Anglicised sense of propriety by wearing hats to the office and ordering Chandler to open windows or adjust Venetian blinds without saying 'please'. (Wilder also took long phone calls from women which irked Chandler, married to the seventy-five year old Cissy with whom he no longer had a sex life.)

Matters reached a head one day when Chandler failed to turn up for work. Two days later, Sistrom received a list of complaints about Wilder, written on a yellow legal pad which he had attached to his clipboard. He expected an apology and a change of working practices or else he would resign. Wilder provided the apology, although disputes continued over the subsequent months it took to complete the script.

Chandler may have achieved this moderate victory over etiquette but he also proved persuasive in stylistic concerns, most notably the use of dialogue. Wilder had initially wanted to retain as much of the original dialogue in the novel as he felt its harsh realism was exactly the voice he wanted to reproduce. However, Chandler felt the dialogue was intended for the eye, not the ear. He wrote to Cain:

> Nothing could be more natural and easy and to the point on paper, and yet it doesn't quite play ... On the screen, this is all lost, and the essential mildness of the phrasing shows up as lacking in sharpness. They tell me that this is the difference between

photographable dialogue and written dialogue. For the screen everything has to be sharpened and pointed and wherever possible eluded.

Double Indemnity, 1992, p. 37

Cain, more experienced, but not as gifted a screenwriter as Chandler agreed with him. When they eventually met, he concurred with Chandler's suggestions. Cain remarked that, 'Chandler, an older man a bit irked by Wilder's omniscience, had this odd little smile on his face as the talk went on'.

The writing was good enough to secure an academy award nomination. Chandler was to reflect in a letter to Hamish Hamilton:

> Working with Billy Wilder on *Double Indemnity* was an agonizing experience and has probably shortened my life, but I learned from it about as much about screenwriting as I am capable of learning, which is not very much. Like every writer, or almost every writer who goes to Hollywood, I was convinced in the beginning that there must be some discoverable method of working in the pictures which would not be completely stultifying to whatever creative talent one might possess. But like others before me I discovered this was a dream ... The wise screenwriter is he who wears his second best suit, artistically speaking, and doesn't take too much to heart.
>
> *10 November, 1950*

Maurice Zolotow, Wilder's biographer, quoted some of Chandler's complaints to him. Whilst Wilder had always been unstinting in his praise of Chandler's writing ability, he was not so compliant when faced with his personal grievances:

> 'Hollywood treated him badly? We didn't invite him to the preview? How could we? He was under a table drunk at Lucey's (a renowned watering hole for dipsomaniac writers). It's a wonder they don't say Hollywood drove him to drink. I've heard people say that I drove him to drink. Don't fall for that dreck – what Hollywood

did to Raymond Chandler. What did Raymond Chandler do to Hollywood?'

Raymond Chandler in Hollywood, 1982

FILMING SCHEDULE

The shooting of the film took place between 27 September and 24 November 1943, a period of less than two months. There were relatively few sets: the inside of the Dietrichson house; Neff's apartment; The Pacific All Risk Insurance Company; and location shooting was limited to the bowling alley, the drive-in, the supermarket, the exterior of the Dietrichson house and the street locations for the car scene at the start of the film.

Wilder has commented on the professionalism of his cast and crew and the fact that no star tantrums slowed down proceedings. In fact, the reverse was true. The main post-production feature was the addition of Miklos Rozsa's ominous and foreboding score which reinforced the mood of fatalism with such conviction (see Style: Sound).

Early previews were extremely successful and Cain felt that Wilder had greatly improved upon his original novel. As we have seen, preview reviews in *Variety* and *The Motion Picture Herald* were extremely positive and reviews upon release in September 1944 showed similar praise and enthusiasm. Playing on the film's advertising slogan Alfred Hitchcock telegrammed Wilder and said, 'Since Double Indemnity the most important words are Billy Wilder'. The film was nominated for seven academy awards, a major achievement for a film which many had said could never be made. Wilder may have lost to more sentimental fare on the evening but the Oscars he received a year later for *The Lost Weekend* perhaps owed something to the pioneering success of *Double Indemnity*.

Despite its critical success, the film did not constitute a major box office success. It made a small profit but did not rank alongside the top grossers of 1944.

INDUSTRIAL

One of the fundamental legal challenges for Wilder and Chandler when writing the screenplay was to produce a script which would placate the

came close to contravening elements of the code

Breen Office, who were extremely doubtful that *Double Indemnity* could be filmed. A self-regulatory code of ethics had been established in 1930 by the Motion Picture Producers and Distributors of America (M.P.P.D.A.) in an attempt to improve the image of the industry. Hays had considerable power as head of the M.P.P.D.A., with Joseph Breen as director of the code administration. The Hays administration itself ended in 1945 but the code remained until 1966, when civil liberty groups influenced a major revision, eventually leading to a ratings system in 1968.

A key tenet of the code which applied to Wilder's film was its conviction that 'no picture shall be made which will lower the standards of those who see it. Hence the sympathy of the audience should never be thrown to the side of crime, wrongdoing, evil or sin'. The ambivalent tone of key scenes in *Double Indemnity* came close to contravening elements of the code and perhaps it is only the fates of the two protagonists which allowed the film to be made. Other regulations which Wilder and Chandler had to remain mindful of included 'Methods of crime should not be explicitly presented' and 'excessive and lustful kissing, lustful embracing, suggestive postures and gesture, are not to be shown'. Some critics have suggested that the film requires more exchanges of passion between Neff and Phyllis to show how sexual obsession forces Neff to become involved in murder, and that censorship may have adversely affected this depiction of character motivation.

Surprisingly, the objections to the completed script were minimal. Wilder was told to ensure that Phyllis's bath towel fully covered her body and to minimise scenes involving Dietrichson's corpse. As methods of crime had to be hidden a line was removed where Neff tells Phyllis not to handle the insurance policy unless she is wearing gloves.

paramount

Paramount was one of the 'big five' Hollywood studios, along with Warner Bros, MGM, RKO and 20th Century Fox. The companies were described as 'vertically integrated' as they controlled distribution and exhibition, along with production. As mentioned previously, Paramount did not have the executive producers who imposed a dominant house style as did the other

paramount

a 'director's studio'

studios and it was regarded as more of a 'director's studio' than any other of the big five.

In the late 1920s and early 1930s production designer Hans Drier and directors like Ernst Lubitsch created a European style which led to commercial success in the domestic and international market. The imminence of war in the late 1930s curtailed the international market and led to significant changes in the roster of stars and directors at the studio.

During Wilder's fertile period key actors on the roster included Ray Miland, Bob Hope, Dorothy Lamour, Paulette Goddard, Barbara Stanwyck and underrated talent such as Fred MacMurray and William Holden who were to elevate to the status of major stars. Wilder's directing contemporaries after his mentor Lubitsch included Mitchell Leisen and Preston Sturges, whose transition from writer to director had influenced Wilder's own development.

The studio had a diverse range of films, with Wilder's film noir and gritty social realism at one extreme and the Hope and Crosby road movies at the other. It was an extremely successful company in Wilder's time and in 1946 its record profits of nearly $40 million were approximately twice that of its competitors.

In 1948, a landmark ruling known as the Paramount Decree forced Paramount and the other majors to relinquish control of the theatre chains which had helped them to control the industry for so long. The subsequent division of the company meant it would never have quite the same control again.

audience

Marxist and psychoanalytical theorists believed that classic Hollywood cinema 'works to interpolate the film spectator binding his or her desire with dominant ideological positions' and 'conceals this ideological process by providing the spectator with the comforting assurance that they are a unified, transcendent, meaning-making subject' (*The Cinema Book*, 1999, p. 366).

audience

Wilder may belong to the Hollywood, naturalistic tradition but he often jars the audience from a fixed position. The fates of the villains in *Double Indemnity* may satisfy the Production Code but the spirit of their depiction does not. We warm to Neff, dislike Dietrichson and share anxiety with the two conspirators when their getaway car fails to start. Everything from casting, music to script conceals moral ambiguities which produces an audience response more complex than the B movies which had characterised previous film noir.

Some debate exists as to whether the audience for classic cinema was middle class or immigrant and working class. Despite claims that nickelodeons were found in middle-class areas, most evidence suggests that the bulk of early audiences came from working class and immigrant viewers. Quite how they found this middle-class crime is debatable. However, the Snyder-Grey case of 1927 did give events of this nature a sensational grounding in real events. The film was a massive critical success although this was not matched at the box office. It did make money, but it was not one of the significant earners of its year.

Nevertheless, the critical stature of the film has grown overtime. Woody Allen has described it as 'practically anybody's best movie' and in an age where many films are undermined by their over-lengthy execution, its tightness, economy and precision are admirable. Contemporary film-makers like Mike Nichols and Martin Scorsese have described Wilder as 'the master' and *Double Indemnity* was the film which marked a turning point in his output and in the status afforded to film noir.

bibliography

general film

Altman, Rick, *Film Genre*,
BFI, 1999
    Detailed exploration of film genres

Bordwell, David, *Narration in the
Fiction Film*, Routledge, 1985
    A detailed study of narrative theory
    and structures

– – –, Staiger, Janet & Thompson,
Kristin, *The Classical Hollywood
Cinema: Film Style & Mode of
Production to 1960*,
Routledge, 1985; pbk 1995
    An authoritative study of cinema as
    institution, it covers film style and
    production

– – – & Thompson, Kristin,
Film Art,
McGraw-Hill, 4th edn, 1993
    An introduction to film aesthetics for
    the non-specialist

Branson, Gill & Stafford, Roy,
The Media Studies Handbook,
Routledge, 1996

Buckland, Warren, *Teach Yourself
Film Studies*, Hodder & Stoughton,
1998
    Very accessible, it gives an overview
    of key areas in film studies

Cook, Pam & Bernink, Mieke, *The
Cinema Book*, BFI, 2nd edn, 1999
    An excellent book. It is encyclopaedic
    in its coverage yet it retains a depth
    of analysis that few texts can match.
    Excellent sections on The American
    Film Industry and Genre

Corrigan, Tim, *A Short Guide To
Writing About Film*, HarperCollins, 1994
    What it says: a practical guide for
    students

Dyer, Richard, *Stars*, BFI, 1979;
pbk Indiana University Press, 1998
    A good introduction to the star
    system

Easthope, Antony, *Classical Film
Theory*, Longman, 1993
    A clear overview of recent writing
    about film theory

Hayward, Susan, *Key Concepts in
Cinema Studies*, Routledge, 1996

Hill, John & Gibson, Pamela Church
(eds), *The Oxford Guide to Film Studies*,
Oxford University Press, 1998
    Wide-ranging standard guide

Lapsley, Robert & Westlake, Michael,
Film Theory: An Introduction,
Manchester University Press, 1994

Maltby, Richard & Craven, Ian,
Hollywood Cinema, Blackwell, 1995
    A comprehensive work on the
    Hollywood industry and its products

Mulvey, Laura, 'Visual Pleasure and
Narrative Cinema' (1974), in *Visual
and Other Pleasures*,
Indiana University Press, Bloomington,
1989
    The classic analysis of 'the look' and
    'the male gaze' in Hollywood cinema.
    Also available in numerous other
    edited collections

Nelmes, Jill (ed.), *Introduction to Film
Studies*, Routledge, 1996
    Deals with several national cinemas
    and key concepts in film study

Nowell-Smith, Geoffrey (ed.),
The Oxford History of World Cinema,
Oxford University Press, 1996
    Hugely detailed and wide-ranging
    with many features on 'stars'

double indemnity

Thomson, David, *A Biographical Dictionary of the Cinema*, Secker & Warburg, 1975
Unashamedly driven by personal taste, but often stimulating

Truffaut, François, *Hitchcock*, Simon & Schuster, 1966, rev. edn, Touchstone, 1985
Landmark extended interview

Turner, Graeme, *Film as Social Practice*, 2nd edn, Routledge, 1993
Chapter four, 'Film Narrative', discusses structuralist theories of narrative

Wollen, Peter, *Signs and Meaning in the Cinema*, Viking, 1972
An important study in semiology

Readers should also explore the many relevant websites and journals. *Film Education* and *Sight and Sound* are standard reading.

Valuable websites include:

The Internet Movie Database at http://uk.imdb.com

Screensite at http://www.tcf.ua.edu/screensite/contents.html

The Media and Communications Site at the University of Aberystwyth at http://www.aber.ac.uk/~dgc/welcome.html

There are obviously many other university and studio websites which are worth exploring in relation to film studies.

double indemnity

Cameron, Ian, *The Movie Book of Film Noir*, Studio Vista, Cassell, 1994

Clark, Al, *Raymond Chandler in Hollywood*, Proteus Books, 1982
Another useful book on Raymond Chandler's life is *Raymond Chandler Speaking*, Four Square Books, 1966

Crowe, Cameron, *Conversations with Wilder*, Alfred A. Knopf, 1999
A fascinating dialogue with the director which gives unrestricted access to his views for the first time. It combines autobiography with invaluable technical insights

Culler, Jonathan, *On Deconstruction*, Routledge and Kegan Paul Ltd, 1982

Evans, Peter William, *Double Indemnity*, BFI, 1994

Kaplan, E. Ann (ed.), *Women in Film Noir*, BFI, 1998
A seminal contribution on gender and film noir. Excellent introduction and significant essays by Janey Place, Sylvia Harvey and Claire Johnston

Metz, Christian, *Film Language, A Semiotics of the Cinema*, OUP Inc, 1974

Sarris, Andrew, *The American Cinema: Directors and Directions, 1929–1968*, New York, Dutton, 1968
See definition of auteur in Cinematic Terms

Schatz, Thomas, *The Genius of the System, Hollywood Film-making in the Studio Era*, Faber and Faber, 1998

Schickel, Richard,
Double Indemnity, BFI Classics, 1992,
reprinted 1993, 1996
   Detailed, informative and genuinely
   illuminating, this book traces the
   literary origins through the
   production history to the critical
   response. This is required reading for
   any student of the film

Schrader, Paul,
Notes on Film Noir,
Film Comment, Spring 1972
   One of the strongest attempts to
   classify and define film noir

Silver, Alain & Ward, Elizabeth,
Film Noir,
Secker and Warburg, 1980

Stam, Robert, Burgogyne, Robert &
Flitterman-Lewis, Sandy,
New Vocabularies in Film Semiotics,
Structuralism, Post-Structuralism and
Beyond, Routledge, 1992

Tuska, John, *Dark Cinema: American*
Film Noir in Cultural Perspective,
Westport, CT: Greenwood Press, 1984

Wilson, Edmund, 'The Boys in the
Back Room' in *Classics and*
Commercials,
New York: Farrar, Straus, 1950
   The first book to look at the literary
   sources of all the noir texts together

Zolotow, Maurice,
Billy Wilder in Hollywood,
New York, Limelight Editions, 1987

cinematic terms

auteur the notion that the director is the auteur or 'author' of a film was first used in the early 1960s by the critic Andrew Sarris in his key work, *The American Cinema: Directors and Directions, 1929–1968*. He had loosely translated ideas developed by the French journal *Cahiers du Cinema* with its advancement of the *politique des auteurs* notion in 1954

chiaroscuro a pointed distinction between light and dark areas of the frame achieved by the use of low-key lighting

continuity editing this creates the illusion of continuity through straight cuts which do not distract us from the action

contrapuntal sound any sound which contrasts strongly with the image on screen

dénouement the unravelling of a plot leading to the final resolution (closure)

diegetic sound any sound which is integral to the world of the film

dissolve an image slowly brought in beneath another image. This is frequently done to register time or spatial shifts in *Double Indemnity*

doppelganger person's ghost or apparition seen shortly before or after his death

ellipsis the deliberate omission of events in the film, possibly to add pace or tension to the narrative

femme fatale a woman with a dangerously attractive sexuality, who could use her seductive powers to empower herself and suborn others to her will. In the Hollywood films of the noir period she was the antithesis of the archetypal domestic woman

film noir the term devised by French critics to describe Hollywood films of the 1940s and 1950s, which depicted the dark underworld of American society, populated by the corrupt, criminal and cynical characters. The films went against the idealism of many other genres such as the western or romantic comedy

flashback a reversal of the temporal flow often used in film noir to give a sense of fatalism as events have already occurred, rendering the protagonists hopeless to the prevailing mood of inevitability

functions a term derived from Propp to describe acts of characters, which have particular significance on the course of action

high-key lighting more filler light is used to create a more realistic effect

low-key lighting the use of only the key and back lights to create the strong contrasts of light and dark, typical of film noir

mise-en-scène this rather elegant term cumbersomely translates as 'what is put into the scene or frame' and clearly that which is included or excluded has considerable impact upon the semantics of film. The visual composition includes lighting, costume, setting, positioning etc.

montage the selection, cutting and piecing together of sections of film as a whole

narratology the theoretical analysis of narrative or the study of a film's realisation and elaboration of a story

cinematic terms

non-diegetic sound a sound imposed externally upon the world of the film. In *Double Indemnity* this is usually the use of music and aspects of Neff's voice-over

parallel sound music or other sound effects which complement the action

shot/reverse shot a series of shots in which the reciprocal gazes of characters are captured through a succession of eye-line to eye-line shots

spheres of action Propp's term for the combination of plot function and tale roles

tale role the term devised by Propp to condense the diverse range of characters in Russian wondertales into seven archetypal figures also referred to as dramatis personae. These figures included: the villain, the donor, the helper, the princess and her father, the dispatcher, the hero and the false hero. These roles were then related by academics to character roles in films such as villain, femme fatale, nurturing wife etc.

temporal and spatial transformations movements in time or space often achieved in *Double Indemnity* via the use of flashback

top lighting a glamorous effect created when the main light source comes from above

wondertale the Russian folk tales used by Propp for the application and development of his narrative theories, which were later deployed by a range of film theorists

credits

production company

Paramount Pictures

location

Los Angeles, California

filming

27 September 1943 –
24 November 1943

running time

107 minutes

US release

7 September 1944

UK release

16 October 1944

director

Billy Wilder

producer

B.G. DeSylva and Joseph Sistrom

screenplay

Billy Wilder and Raymond
Chandler from the novel *Double
Indemnity* by James M. Cain

photography

John Seitz

supervising editor

Doane Harrison

art director

Hans Dreier, Hal Pereira

music

Miklos Rozsa, based on Cesar
Franck's Symphony in D minor

song

'Tangerine' by Victor Schertzinger,
Johnny Mercer

cast

Walter Neff – Fred MacMurray

Phyllis Dietrichson –
Barbara Stanwyck

Barton Keyes –
Edward G. Robinson

Lola Dietrichson – Jean Heather

Mr Dietrichson – Tom Powers

Nino Zachetti – Byron Barr

Edward S. Norton Jr –
Richard Gaines

Mr Jackson – Porter Hall

Sam Gorlopis – Fortunio Bonanova

Nennie the maid –
Betty Farrington

Charlie, garage attendant –
Sam McDaniel

Other titles in the series

Other titles available in the York Film Notes series:

Title	ISBN
8½ (Otto e mezzo)	0582 40488 6
A bout de souffle	0582 43182 4
Apocalypse Now	0582 43183 2
Battleship Potemkin	0582 40490 8
Blade Runner	0582 43198 0
Casablanca	0582 43201 4
Chinatown	0582 43199 9
Citizen Kane	0582 40493 2
Das Cabinet des Dr Caligari	0582 40494 0
Dracula	0582 43197 2
Easy Rider	0582 43195 6
Fargo	0582 43193 X
Fear Eats the Soul	0582 48224 3
La Haine	0582 43194 8
Lawrence of Arabia	0582 43192 1
Psycho	0582 43191 3
Pulp Fiction	0582 40510 7
Romeo and Juliet	0582 43189 1
Some Like It Hot	0582 40503 3
Stagecoach	0582 43187 5
Taxi Driver	0582 40506 8
The Full Monty	0582 43181 6
The Godfather	0582 43188 3
The Piano	0582 43190 5
The Searchers	0582 40510 6
The Terminator	0582 43186 7
The Third Man	0582 40511 4
Thelma and Louise	0582 43184 0
Unforgiven	0582 43185 9

Also from York Notes

Also available in the **York Notes** range:

York Notes
The ultimate literature guides for GCSE students (or equivalent levels)

York Notes Advanced
Literature guides for A-level and undergraduate students (or equivalent levels)

York Personal Tutors
Personal tutoring on essential GCSE English and Maths topics

Available from good bookshops.
For full details, please visit our website at www.longman-yorknotes.com

notes